AF708949

Family, Friends and Other Bleeders

– DEREK HAUGHTON –

An environmentally friendly book printed and bound in England by
www.printondemand-worldwide.com

Mixed Sources
Product group from well-managed forests, and other controlled sources
www.fsc.org Cert no. TT-COC-002641
© 1996 Forest Stewardship Council
FSC

PEFC Certified
This product is from sustainably managed forests and controlled sources
www.pefc.org
PEFC
PEFC/16-33-415

This book is made entirely of chain-of-custody materials

FastPrint Publishing

www.fast-print.net/store.php

FAMILY, FRIENDS AND OTHER BLEEDERS

Cover artwork by Michael Rees

A catalogue record for this book is available from the British Library

ISBN 978-178456-243-4

Also available as
Hardback: ISBN 978-178456-244-1
ePub e-book: ISBN 978-178456-910-5
Mobi e-book: ISBN 978-178456-911-2

First published 2015 by
FASTPRINT PUBLISHING
Peterborough, England.

Preface

This book completes my autobiographical trilogy the first being What Are Yer? Bleeder, from early childhood to leaving education, the second, The Rest of Me Bleeding Life almost up to present time and this last, as the title indicates is less about me and more about those I've met, heard tell of or owe my existence to. In the first book I unfortunately maligned as 'blisteringly dull' one of the only two books kept in my childhood home. Retrieved from bombed-out stock of a bookshop this was too sophisticated a volume for a child. Penalties Upon Opinion by Hypathia Bradlaugh Bonner was in fact a book listing various 'crimes' against the blasphemy laws, a blast against the misery of Christianity which I have now read.

Family history research has filled in a few gaps but much of what is here concerning my family is hearsay, stories I have retained since childhood when my father in particular recounted events in his past and the doings of other family members mostly over and over again. I don't claim to have a memory approaching photographic and consequently may have misplaced chronologically or forgotten certain episodes but have retained a great deal.

The life of a person born with a chronic illness whatever it may be, for me severe haemophilia B, is no more enthralling or compelling than any other but the challenges faced and the necessary adaptations to the reality faced may at least amuse. More importantly the persons and their experiences, most of them now gone, deserve a mention before being subsumed under the overlay that is officially taught history.

Family, Friends & Other Bleeders!

An exhaustive list of all the influential characters in my life would be an exhausting waste of paper and a tedious read so only the fortunate (unfortunate?) few are made examples of! Be warned, there are no conventionally good or bad cardboard cut-outs lurking in these pages but others like me and you seeking to make sense of their journey through a contingent world.

The early influences of home life offer a coherent at least view of life but for a chronically ill child often away from home in hospital or residential school counter views are presented which together with the disruptive nature of the condition provoked, in me, exasperation with hum-drum life as she is lived. In an attempt to placate or at least enable acceptance of my place in the scheme of things I'd be told 'It's the same for everybody.' but as I didn't consider myself a constituent of 'everybody' or an adjunct to anybody this only served to render me even more exasperated. I was very fond of and in some cases loved the people in my life but never felt included, or wished to be included, in any exclusive group unlike my mother for whom family meant all.

Even a committed misanthrope needs others and I was never that only certain that the only 'club' I wanted to belong to was one organised by a self, desperate to protect individuality from interference and control by others. The people and incidents are included in roughly chronological order as the haemophiliac boy moves on through the years learning and discarding as he goes the child and increasingly the man alien to me now and looked back on with compassion.

Enough of the introspective, here the more interesting characters in the drama line up, starting with other haemophiliacs.

Brian Bidmead was never a friend but a companion on many in-patient spells in various hospitals as, thrown together, similar in age, both haemophiliacs and both regulars on the wards we cooperated for survival.

During one afternoon when time was dragging for him he continually tried to gain my attention while I fought to ignore him and read. After vainly trying to annoy me into leaving my book he moaned that he would like to write a letter but had no- one to write to and could I suggest one of the girls I knew. The day before he'd seen me writing a letter and now decided to pester me until in desperation I gave him a cousin's name and address. It was a strange whim for him to light on and I should have known his plan was to irritate me further. I regretted my weakness for as soon as he had the relevant information he started uttering crudities and obscenities that he was going to write. I ignored him, I doubted that he would write it or get it posted or that he was capable of writing or reading never having seen him open a book or been allowed peace to read one myself in his company. I expected him to tease me with a string of badly spelt obscenities, waving it under my nose and telling me to look what he was sending to my cousin under my name or to pass it to a nurse saying he'd caught me writing it. Off it went though, and as there were no unfortunate consequences perhaps it had been innocuous enough. What still puzzles me is what happened to the letter I sent, which never arrived.

It was a hot summer and one of the last times I spent in hospital with Bidmead. One of the younger nurses, a religioso, attempted to interest me and Bidmead in her faith; she ran some kind of Sunday school and gave us each a badge, mine had a picture of a lion and the legend Be Strong and of a Good Courage. Also she sang a little song the tune now lost but here's the gist of the words: Don't be like a coffee pot, coffee pots are tall and thin, be like a teapot and let the sunshine in. It's true the words make no sense as rendered but I feel my version is pretty close. Nevertheless a peculiar little rhyme, whether it was hers or not I can't say. Bidmead was mildly contemptuous but I wore that badge for the rest of my stay and kept it for many years, she was after all trying to help in a sincere though misguided way and I felt slightly sorry for her.

Her other good deed neither of us felt in the least sceptical of, she made us milkshakes, a glass of milk with an ice cream and orange juice whizzed up in a blender, delicious and most welcome, it was a very hot summer indeed.

I never saw Brian at all after leaving school and just a couple of years later my mother came in with the news that he was dead. She'd met his mother in town and been told of his death and the circumstances of the accident that killed him. He and his boisterous mates had rushed down the stairs on a bus that was still moving, no doors on buses then, and he'd fallen off the platform striking his head on the tarmac and suffered a brain haemorrhage from which he died saying over and over oh my head! I was saddened as he and I had shared in the difficulties associated with haemophilia, though not really friends, but what had happened was no surprise as he never took much care.

Other haemophiliacs I knew and had spent time in hospital with were Michael Redeson a friend and one of the gang who haunted the library at school and his cousin Charlie Iverson who I don't remember from school but frequently met in hospital until the family moved to Wales. We three, plus Bidmead, were roughly the same age and so were frequently thrown together. Three younger members of the haemophilia clan were known to me, two brothers and their cousin. The curious thing is that once my parents sold up and moved to Cornwall the cousin and his parents bought the house, further to that sometime previously his cousins the two young brothers had moved to a house further up and on the same side of my street! I think the two boys must have had moderate haemophilia as their joints didn't seem to be damaged by bleeds.

Michael it was who prompted me to go to Oxford Haemophilia Centre for care after we coincided together for the last time in a Coventry hospital. Coventry and Warwick on an orthopaedic ward where I can't be sure why I was there and don't remember what problem Michael had. We were in separate parts of the ward, he in a four-bedder and me in the long ward. A nurse came to me and told me he'd asked if any other haemophiliacs were in and when told yes he asked could we be accommodated together, told yes he asked the nurse to check whether I would agree but to be careful because I was very sarcastic. His assessment came as a surprise, cynical or mildly sardonic I would have accepted without any qualms but sarcasm was not habitual. He needn't have worried I was only too pleased to move to the four-bedder and meet with a familiar old friend.

I still carried into hospital my tin of necessities including analgesics in case those offered were inadequate, sticking plasters, stubs of pencil, safety pins, needle and thread and a teaspoon amongst other useful things and a curious small metal disc from a long-gone toy which when held on end between the front teeth and breathed out through made a strange and penetrating zooming whistle. Impossible to spot unless in the know. I enjoyed the confusion it caused when blown but only did so sparingly. What is that noise? No-one ever found out! Other friends visited me Al included so it was quite a reunion though we'd all only recently left school. Prior to Michael's admission the next bed contained an elderly man Mr Homer who had suffered an accident, breaking a leg, treated to a full length plaster cast he was on traction. Whether it was drugs for the pain or a fever I don't know but he was more or less off his head.

The traction system used had scaffolding poles at the four corners of the bed with parallels joining them, a bar across the foot with weights and a pulley. This elderly man with a broken leg STOOD UP and strode down the bed, whereupon the weights crashed down to the floor and then as he propelled himself backwards by pushing on the parallels the weights smashed back up on to the pulley and cross bar. He travelled up and down repeating the trick with a big grin on his face and shouts of joy. What he thought he was doing and where he thought he was is a mystery but he looked like a little boy enjoying a new toy. In no time a bunch of staff, nurses an SHO and sister were running backwards and forwards with and below urging him to stop and lie back down. To have them joining in only spurred him on to even more joyful exertion until quite suddenly he stopped and did as he was told with a look both fearful and uncertain.

He suffered no trauma from the unauthorised and inadvisable exercise and the event was never repeated much to my disappointment as I'd enjoyed the spectacle almost as much as his exuberance suggested he'd revelled in providing it.

Later that same night as I tried to sleep a rumbling noise came nearer and nearer until under the partition past the beds and out under the opposite partition trundled a set of false teeth! Amazing that they had been bowled along the ward's length staying together as an item and strange that no-one followed to retrieve them.

I was back in the clutches of Mr Bizzaro the orthobod, as at the age of eighteen I was no longer Mr Parry-William's patient. I'd been promised that someone else would be found to take over my care but reverting to Bizzaro appeared to be my fate. It turned out that the sister on this ward knew the sister at Paybody hell-hole and she said 'so you're one of sister Asslik's boys are you?' I refrained from telling her what I thought of the woman and the hospital.

A couple of years later I went to visit Michael at his family home but this visit wasn't altogether a success, he referred to me or the visit as a blast from the past and we didn't plan to meet again. I occasionally heard news of him as my mother knew so many people including his who passed on information. At one point he married and fairly quickly the couple divorced, to mention the reasons behind it would only be to perpetuate gossip so I won't go into what we were told. Michael had some years previously developed inhibitory antibodies produced by the immune system as a response to the factor viii used to treat his condition being mistaken as harmful thus treating his episodes of bleeding becomes more of a problem, requiring the use of bypass agents; how effective, if available, these were back in the nineteen eighties I don't know but I was told the inhibitors were disastrous for him.

Chapter 2

Controlling the subsequent bleed after he slipped and fell on a garage forecourt proved impossible and he died. This too is hearsay but in this case I feel justified in trusting in its veracity. I felt an affinity with Michael although we didn't see eye to eye in some matters, and I remain thankful that we shared friendship for so many years and grateful that I haven't developed inhibitors, less likely for a patient with haemophilia B but still a possibility.

I was astonished by him on two occasions. On learning that I now had a football season ticket he scornfully asked me why I liked football, telling me I could never play so why the interest; this attitude seemed as silly as asking why I liked bird watching when I couldn't fly and the day he told me that if ever there was a cure for haemophilia he would take it and go out and deliberately pick a fight with someone. Both attitudes were crazy to me, if I chose not to like something simply for the reason he gave I might have to dislike so much my life would be impoverished and as for fighting I would do that anyway if it came to the point where I couldn't avoid it and would look for the sharpest or heaviest weapon and use it first. Fighting as a pastime just didn't appeal to me, nothing to do with haemophilia.

Michael did the right thing and took a job that paid him only for the hours he actually worked, these days known as a zero-hours contract but then a rarity, but the right thing because any job is better than none, right? So for him back then no holiday pay, or sick pay when a bleed meant time off, just the money he earned from the hours worked. I heard of this arrangement not from Michael but when the suggestion was made that I should do the same.

No, no, no not this Dek boy (as another old friend would say) I wasn't about to add a further measure of suspense into a life already uncertain. My chief difficulty in life up until then wasn't the actual bleeds into knees and elbows but the knowledge that I could never say for sure in the morning that I'd be fit for anything by the evening and the addition of financial uncertainty would have reduced me to a permanently anxious and ultimately depressed state. So I did the wrong thing instead choosing to live with the certainty of penury.

Although I had developed a policy for living or a personal philosophy that allowed me to thrive in my own way with elements of Marxism, existentialism, Buddhist thinking and hedonism, all were and are tempered with a heavy coating of pragmatism.

Advice Michael once gave me I chose to ignore, he offered me a small cigar telling me it would settle my nerves, I wasn't particularly nervous and if I had been I would not have tried self-medication but I took it and kept it just in case 'nerves' began to trouble me. Later as it dried and started to break up I threw it away.

I did smoke cigarettes for a time, once married to Alice everyone around me smoked and viewed me with something like suspicion when I refused the regularly proffered packet. I adopted the 'when in Rome' position but gave it up on the realisation that the pleasure felt was down to the relief from craving that I wouldn't have had if I'd never ignited the chemical larded remains of tortured leaves in the first place..

Lighting up felt good because it stopped me feeling bad, so I got feeling bad over in one go and quit the damn things. No more asking if people minded my smoking in their presence, making sure I had both cigarettes and lighter or matches, no longer beset by the stink or finding it necessary to waste money on something ridiculous.

I won't say it was easy to give up the silly habit; it took several false starts until I examined the problem in detail. What gave me a clue was hearing an acquaintance say he was about to try to give up, but he said, if I start to get ratty with the wife and kids I'll start again. From this statement I expected two things, that his wife and kids were going to suffer and that he would then give up the attempt. A few days later he described just that and let me know he was proud of his actions 'At least I tried.' There we have it! He had tried to give up smoking and if you set out to try you can't lose, any fool can try. Don't let yourself try, as Charles Bukowski's gravestone advises Don't Try, instead do it and stick to it, the addiction generates good reasons why you should start again, don't entertain them, dismiss them as soon as they enter and do something other than light up, soon enough they'll become a thing of the past and you will have won, as I did.

Michael's cousin very soon after moving to Wales was required to use a wheelchair full time and later I heard without knowing the circumstances that he too had died.

So of the four contemporary haemophiliacs only I survived into middle-age. The elder of the three younger haemophiliacs known to me developed another serious health problem when he became unsteady on his feet, falling dangerously and multiple sclerosis was diagnosed, extremely bad luck pointing to the truth that no immunity to other disasters is conferred on anyone coping with a chronic illness.

My mother Grace Edna Hamlet was born on the fourteenth of March 1909 at 2, Crosslands Row, Burbage Leicestershire. Hinckley, closely adjacent, the market town where she spent most of her childhood she referred to as 'Tin 'At' (Tin Hat) and Burbage, Soppy Land, this said with a rueful smile as she'd been teased with her birthplace as a child. By the time she reached sixteen both parents were dead. Her father Joshua dying when she was only nine years old, her mother Harriet (Lal) seven years later. These recorded dates do not agree with my memory of what she told me however 'Dad died when I was seven and Mum when I was fourteen.' though it is possible that it's my mistake having focussed on the seven in the story. I know that she was traumatised by the death of her mother, so that when employed as a farm servant she had to be reminded that she had no parents to write home to; it would not be a surprise if she was a little hazy about the dates. Her memories of her parents were all fond and she would tell me of her father coming home after a drink or two and throwing his cap in at the door saying 'If tha cooms out I must stay out, if tha stays in I can coom in.' Her smile as she told me this meant that she'd realised that it was in fun. She would show me a photograph of Hinckley Sunday School Treat, a march with banners flying, and would point to a little girl easy to distinguish as all the others are dressed in white and her in mourning.

Joshua Hamlet was born 1847 in Rotherham Yorkshire and Harriet my maternal grandmother was his second wife; his first marriage to Emma Jane Webster had ended with her death in 1889 leaving their three children motherless, the youngest, Benjamin, having a Burbage address in 1901 suggests that he moved down with his father at only twelve years old. His other two children Richard E was recorded as a lodger in Yorkshire and Martha A as a servant. Unfortunately, I know little else about my maternal grandfather apart from his aversion to anyone wearing green, Mum led me to believe an Irish connection existed in the ancestry of one of her parents so was that a Northern Irish Protestant one?

He died in 1918 many years before my birth so I can only speculate on his frame of mind when his first wife died, the children were split up and taken care of as best as could be managed. Was he devastated by Emma's death or were they not overly close? Did he keep in touch with the children regularly and how and where did he meet Lal his next wife?

Harriet Mary Wright was born Carlton Notts. 1861 and died aged sixty-four, the mother of ten children in 1925. Given the prevailing poverty and the pre NHS shortcomings in health provision, together with ten full-term pregnancies, sixty-four was a reasonably long life for a woman given that the overall life expectancy was under sixty. This was a lady of determination, who made her decisions and stood by them through situations where many would have allowed authority and society in general to paralyse them with shame and remorse. I like to think we would have got on well if our time here had coincided.

In contrast to Dad I know little of Mum's childhood as she spoke of it rarely in comparison and some of what she told me she either couldn't or wouldn't elaborate on.

She had an elder brother, Alfie, who died aged only fourteen and in Mum's words 'Had something wrong with his legs and didn't go to school, your Gran taught him at home. He was clever, just like you.' A flattering assessment of me intellectual prowess and as one always susceptible to flattery I've remembered the words verbatim. Harriet had been a governess, according to Mum, so was well qualified to teach her son. The governess part of the story might not be correct however; perhaps Mum meant only that she acted as a governess teaching Alfie. Memory plays tricks at times and mine is not immune from the disorder. It may well be that I elaborated on the story to account for what took place prior to Alfie's birth; big house, governess seduced and cast aside, son banished to oversee sugar cane production on some remote island. The standard novelistic stuff, brutal or over-sentimentalised……..Hmm, sounds promising!

Chapter 3

A banal explanation, less romance more tragedy is closer to the truth but whatever the circumstances I shall never know. Alfie's lifelong health problem was not directly to blame for his early death, again my mother's words: He died of the colly brawn, it was his favourite and Mum got it for a treat. Quizzed as to how pressed meat could have killed him she would shrug and say 'I don't know, all I know is it killed him'. She was passing on only what she'd been told as the poor boy died before she was born. The facts I have gathered support what she told me and add a further air of misfortune to both the short life of Alfie and that of my grandmother.

He died 9th November 1901, registered at death Alfred Wright Hamlet, curiously the certificate gives cause of death as 'Syncope, due to ptomaine poisoning, accidental death. Does the 'accidental death' clause mean a coroner's inquest? I don't claim to be a medic but syncope is surely fainting, so he fainted to death? As a non-medic here's my opinion, definitely secondary; he suffered quick onset food-poisoning, most probably the brawn being contaminated with e-coli, and he actually died from dehydration occasioned by vomiting and diarrhoea and that his 'fainting' was in fact a coma. Whatever his abiding medical condition before consuming the brawn it may have weakened his defences. His mother bought the brawn as a treat for her housebound son, how unfortunate for him and how devastating for her.

Alfred Wright was born 28th. December 1887 in Basford Workhouse Nottinghamshire, no father is recorded. What circumstances had left Harriet Mary, no young girl emerging from childhood but twenty-six years old and probably viewed as an aging spinster at the time, friendless and abandoned to give birth just three days after the Christmas celebrations I have been unable to ascertain. As this is no fictionalised account all I can have is admiration for poor Harriet, pregnant and reduced to the workhouse, a place deliberately imbued with horror by authority and viewed as such by the working population. The pressure to name the father must have been intense, the manufactured shame and condemnatory ridicule of the loving pious hard to resist. Who knows what struggles she and her son endured to stay together an unmarried mother and a disabled child, who helped? her parents, the Salvation Army or, unlikely as it seems the father of the child? I have been unable to ascertain any information concerning where when or how mother and child lived until the security offered by marriage to Joshua.

Her next child Blanche Ethel – always known as Ethel – was born after the marriage when Alfie would have been six/seven. As indicated what happened during the years between the two births remains lost. As to Joshua he lodged at a house in Leicester after the death of his first wife according to the 1891 census and ten years later was married to Harriet with three daughters, the eldest six years and an 'adopted' son. Harriet has eluded me in the above mentioned census so her whereabouts prior to marriage remain unknown. The Salvation Army played a part in the life of the daughters including my mother hence the possibility Harriet may have been helped by them? After the disaster of giving birth in the workhouse, alone and without a marriage certificate she would certainly have needed help.

After the death of Joshua, caring for the family, keeping the home together and coping with the younger children, including three boys provided a further challenge.

The sons, in particular Ted, my brother Syd's favourite uncle who was a terror as a boy in the area of Hinckley where the family lived, must have led Harriet a merry dance after the death of his father. Mum used to tell of one errant soul terrorised into back-tracking after crying 'I'm the king' when some game requiring such a droll character who quickly changed his mind when Ted glared at him and asked '*Who's* the king?' and yelled Teddy Hamlet's the king, Teddy Hamlet's the king!' When the boys included Mum in their fun it was as a handy dupe as when Ted sat her on a high window-sill and instructed her to hold on to a length of strong, black thread stretched across the street. 'Be a good girl and don't let go?' The boys then retired to a safe distance and watched. Mum was proud to be given such an obviously important role in the boy's game and sat tight as a figure turned the corner and paced importantly up the street. The policeman's head jerked back as the chinstrap prevented his helmet from bouncing to the ground behind him and the boys disappeared round the opposite corner. Mum was upset because the thread had been pulled from her hand and she'd promised to hold on to it. She was only a very little girl and quite innocent of the 'crime' so the policeman helped her down and took her home and the boys received a fitting punishment not least for using their little sister and leaving her to face the copper's wrath alone.

Money was scarce; Harriet had to take in washing to support her family and after her experience of the workhouse poor relief was anathema. To feed such a large family must have been a struggle. One mealtime when the food was being dished up one of the boys started to cry; Harriet asked him what he was crying for and he replied 'I don't want you to have any.' An outrageous response no doubt but with so little to go round one less mouth to feed meant more for the rest.

A minor mystery concerns the middle name of another brother William Hewitt, who in common with most of his siblings used his middle name; in his case shortened to Hughie. Where did Hewitt come from? Mum told me, but always seemed quite vague about the details, that he had a different name to the rest of them.

There must have been a deal of jealousy within the family as I have an early photograph of Mum and someone has scratched out the eyes. When I asked her about it she said one of the lads had been jealous but she couldn't remember which.

Of her school days she told me little but could still recite verses that she had learned concerning a monkey, to my sorrow I recall only a few words:

Master Pat was a monkey
A mischievous monkey too.

These were the first two lines. I remember the rhyme in the fourth line was glue and that the amusive simian inadvertently consumed, at some point, mustard. Mustard was achieved rather than spoken, by which I mean she acted as she'd been taught all those years before with a dramatic pause before the word and great emphasis in pronunciation involving a nod of the head. I wish I had the whole poem here at least and at best a video of her performing it.

If she told me more about school I haven't retained it. The games she mentioned were shuttlecock and battledore better known these days as badminton, also diablo. She played in the local park, this I know because she told me that there was a Great War tank on display there; she never went near it and the local council were compelled to remove it as, in her words: It stank. All the lads used to pee in it, the dirty devils!

She joined the Life Saving Guards, a Salvation Army youth group and took part in displays of Indian club swinging, popular events at the time and an approved form of healthy group exercise and during one display received a broken nose, not from contact with a swung club but due to the attentions of a follower of Baden-Powell. 'There were lots of us from all over, on the playing field, scouts as well and a couple of them took a fancy to me and my friend and came running over to the bench where we were sitting; as he sat down one of them accidentally poked me in the nose with this scout pole he was carrying, ooh it didn't half hurt and bleed, he broke my nose and I thought well, if that's how the lads treat you they can keep away.' Her perceiving of the episode as salutary may have helped to convince her of the efficacy of corporal punishment, as she thought it a good way to counter petty crime. She told me 'There were two lads down the street, when I was a girl; they were always getting the birch'. The fact that repeated beatings failed to prevent further bouts of disapproval rousing behaviour was lost on her. Still society had its revenge and perhaps the crude example discouraged other potential miscreants at least those who learned the lesson that authority was to be despised for its heavy hand.

On the death of Harriet the orphaned family members still at home were organised by Aunt Flo, and Mum was found a live-in job, 'in service' living within her employer's home.

Chapter 4

Mum was sent to a farm as a general servant, where she was treated very fairly by the family for whom she worked and spoke of those times as generally happy and the family supportive and kind.

Once a month the live - in farm servants were required to write home to their parents and when the time came around Mum sat down with the others and picked up a pen, the farmer's wife asked her what she was doing 'Writing to Mum and Dad.' She had somehow put it out of her mind that they were dead but was gently reminded when told 'I'm sorry Grace, you don't have a Mum and Dad any more'. I hope and expect she was encouraged to write to her sister instead but this was not part of the story.

My mother always referred to herself as stubborn as indeed she was, also secretive and on occasion manipulative, although if she realised the latter traits she never said.

She had worked at the farm only a short time before developing a problem with her knees which became a little swollen and quite stiff overnight but cleared up as the morning wore on. She chose to hide these symptoms taking her time to come down to breakfast and exercising until some of the stiffness wore off. Her employers never suspected as was her intention fearing she would be sent away if they found out and after a couple of months the symptoms disappeared as mysteriously as had their onset, never to return.

Curiously at a slightly later age I had similar knee problems that I referred to as pseudo - bleeds waking in the morning with a swollen and stiff knee, sometimes both but without pain unlike an actual bleed. The application of firmly wound crepe bandages helped and by mid - morning the swelling and stiffness disappeared. A knee bleed would simply have got worse and the pain agonising. I kept the news of this new bodily phenomenon to myself not wanting further hospital appointments, investigations and treatment and in a few months whatever it was fizzled out.

Her manipulation of events tended to be well planned as in this episode. She liked biscuits and was especially fond of custard creams but when the biscuit barrel was handed round for everyone to take one she refused. When all were sleeping she would creep down the stairs and help herself to two or three. The repeated theft was discovered and servants and children brought together for the purpose of exposing the culprit, 'Grace may go about her duties, she doesn't care for custard creams'.

One of her duties was to search for hen's eggs that had been 'laid away', certain of the free - range hens would lay their eggs under hedges and these would be searched for and added to the total for sale, this she objected to so any found would be surreptitiously smashed as it was impossible to tell how long they'd been there.

Stubborn when the unspeakable hunting the uneatable came along and the master of the hunt ordered her to open a gate for him. 'You girl, open the gate!' How surprised this 'gentleman' was to be told 'I shan't then, if you want it opened get off your horse and open it yourself'.

He blustered at her but being sure of her ground she continued to refuse. Red in the face he did as advised and threatening her with 'I'll see that your employer hears of this' took himself and his mount off to wherever such types go when they go. A couple of days later she was taken aside by the farmer and asked for her side of the story, when she explained he calmly told her 'Now Grace, never be rude to anyone but you were quite right not to open the gate, you work for me not him.' From this I infer that he owned the land he farmed and was not a tenant to be bullied by a landlord.

One evening, after foraging for pignuts, the tuber of the plant conopodium majus which she loved to eat, she left it late and walking up the lane after twilight but before full dark she was pursued by a screaming something and taking a terrified glance over her shoulder she saw in the gloom a ghost rushing through the air with outstretched arms. As she put it 'I flew down the lane and didn't stop running until back at the farm'. The ghost was of course a barn owl she was informed with friendly laughter but she made sure from then on to get home before dark.

My own encounters with birdlife were mostly positive although not without regret and frustration, a long term starling study abandoned through hospitalisation, two pet budgerigars one after the other that I worried about as they should have been with their own kind, several rescued pets and racing pigeons returned to their owners and a fledged sparrow I tried and failed to save.

Only once have I had a close friendship with a wildling, a hen blackbird whose trust over a couple of years was complete, feeding on proprietary seed at my feet, watching me mix mud for her nest after I noticed she was taking soil from watered plant pots and then using it to build under the bungalow veranda. A full account of our 'relationship' and other wildlife experiences will be made available in my next projected book Nature and Me, but an indication of the trust may be judged from this. I was forking over one of my four foot square vegetable beds and rested my arm then noticed my hand was just three inches from her back as she waited for me to turn up an edible insect or worm. She didn't flinch when I lifted my arm and stayed around until the bed was done.

My only other contact was with my two budgies. Both unimaginatively named Joey but as different in personality and accomplishments as any of my family. Both turned out to be female once the cere coloured and both were great friends. Joey two could be irritating as she kept her eye on me at all times and if I looked towards her cage she would start running back and forth along the perch feathers flat to her body and I would feel obliged to go to her even though engaged on something else at the time. I had a shed at the bottom of the garden with a window that looked directly towards the house but even at that range if I looked up from reading or writing she noticed and started to rush up and down. I learned not to look! Joey one would spin her toy fairground wheel around as you counted, one she would with a flick of her beak spin the wheel, two again and keep it up as long as you carried on counting. She was the first one I looked for on arriving home from school each day, a mistake as it turned out and one day she was lying dead in the bottom of her cage. For a time I had been greeted by Mum with the words 'Bird's dead.' and before I could check, my heart thumping she'd add 'Can't you hear it whistling.' I didn't complain I was becoming, at the age of thirteen, someone who was learning not to react although keeping my temper and contempt under control was still a hard task. I see now that she was probably jealous of the attachment.

Like all of us mother had her faults and the loss of two infants prior to my birth and my haemophilia contributed to her investing too much emotion in our relationship. Overprotection of a child saddled with a chronic illness who resented the input of the adult world and the love each felt for the other made for an 'interesting' battle of wills, I, stubborn in my struggle to maintain independence and Mum equally stubborn in her own methods of attack and defence.

Her technique when other forms of evasion failed she described thus: If anybody got on to me about anything I'd cry at them and they'd feel sorry for me and leave me alone. I can vouch for quality of the acting, the slump of the shoulders, the heavy sobs and screwed up face, even a few tears; the problem with telling me was that at she was bound to utilise it in an attempt to trick me into letting her off the hook at a later date. Sure enough it happened when she came to stay for a few weeks holiday many years later, no need to go into the circumstances apart from the fact that I confronted her with something. She went into full production and after briefly marvelling at the performance I said 'Stop that pretend crying, I know all about it remember? The transformation was instant, from abject wretch to grumbling irritation. 'Well, you shouldn't have mentioned anything.' This from a woman who a second before had been the epitome of misery yet now in a blink sat composed and sulky.

She was well liked at the farm so probably never had to 'cry at them' but she became too well liked by the farmer's son who talked love and proposed marriage. She refused him. The boy's parents tried to persuade her by asking could she not see what a good young man he was and that he loved her? The farm would in the course of time pass to the son and in the meantime there was an available cottage, still she refused and decided to leave the farm. She went to stay with an elder sister near Twycross, North Warwickshire but the sister's relationship with her husband was not good and the atmosphere too unstable besides she didn't like or trust the husband so she packed her suitcase, waved goodbye to her sister Daisy and walked along the canal tow-path to Coventry. She must have set out very early as it would be very difficult to accomplish in one day, a huge undertaking for a young woman requiring strength of purpose and determination to succeed, stubborn in this too and I regret that I never asked her more, including where the idea came from.

Chapter 5

On reaching Coventry she found accommodation with a Mrs Dann in Little Butcher Row. Rooms were let to young women who appear to have been quite boisterous, too much so for Aunt Flo who declared that her sister could not be allowed to live around women 'of that sort.' I think she must have turned up as someone was chanting the rhyme the girls had made about Mrs. Dann:

Old Nelly Dann, she doesn't give a damn
She lifts up her petticoat and pees like a man.

This would certainly have been outrageously vulgar to my aunt as she and the other girls in the family were all Salvationists, Aunt Flo remaining a member for the rest of her life but the others dropping out at various times. Aunt Flo then arranged for Mum to stay with relatives in the city who treated her unfairly as they took money for her upkeep but fed her next to nothing, when they had meat they gave her only the gravy.

On arrival in Coventry Mum had found herself a job in one of the many factories so was able to pay her way and such was her life until she met my father, when on his finding out that she was being more or less starved he asked his mother to make room for her and she moved in as a lodger. I have no idea what Aunt Flo felt about this but suppose she may have thought her duty done and that her sister was now old enough to make her own decisions.

The factory, in common with so many, had guards fitted to the machines and also in common with many, to earn a living wage on piecework a blind eye was turned by management to the removal of guards by machinists. What the guards in fact protected were the owners when in the event of an accident it would be said that the guard provided had been removed without permission. Almost inevitably she had such an accident.

Her left arm became gouged by a machine at the inside quite close to the elbow; on lifting the arm to view the damage and seeing the torn flesh and sinew hanging and the blood pouring down, her only response was 'whatever have I done?' Several of the other girls fainted and off she went to hospital. 'All the guides were hanging out of my arm but it didn't hurt until after they'd seen to it, but ohh, it did throb then. I couldn't sleep.' The surgeon did a very good job to leave her with a usable arm and hand although three fingers were incapable of fully straightening and once the wound healed she coped with all she had to do as though nothing had happened but the scar was a horror of swirling tightened skin. The owners must have been well pleased as the no guard trick did its job and saved them the distress of paying compensation.

Where my parents met I don't recall but I was told a little about the event. Dad and his mate George Edkins spotted Mum across the room, crowded or not, and both were smitten,' she's mine' said George 'she's a virgin!' This being a prime selling point for most men at the time when casting around for a marriage partner, still is no doubt, in some quarters, for myself virginity always seemed a drawback, an impediment requiring too much responsibility in the removal, but happily it takes all sorts.......

The pair engaged her in conversation and Mum was much taken with Dad's curly hair. George put himself out of the running when asked what he did for a living, he smirked the reply 'I make little tin arseholes for little tin dolls' if this was meant to be a joke virginal young ladies would be sure to find amusing and endearing it begs the question what kind of virgin he'd experienced before. No, George was too coarse an individual to appeal to a young woman brought up in a household committed to Salvation Army principles and who never swore, didn't drink alcohol, didn't smoke and refused to wear make-up. Perhaps these things added up to virginity in George's understanding, poor boy, but although George could be very funny and more charming than is readily apparent from the above, Dad's 'lovely curly hair', won the day.

George, at the time, had a street pitch selling the local newspaper for a living and Dad often repeated to me how when he asked George who sold the Midland Daily Telegraph what his unintelligible bellow meant, the answer was 'Tellyonger -and how's-yer-fatherrr!'. My parents would talk of George with regret and tell how he'd died aged only 32 in the blitz along with so many others, and was found standing in a gap between two closely positioned buildings without a mark, lungs collapsed from bomb blast and Mum would sigh and say 'Ah, poor George'.

Syd and Grace married November 1929 and their first child, my brother, also Syd, was born the following October. What their domestic arrangements were at this time I don't know but by June 1932 the family were living in Church Lane with a two month old daughter, Freda, who calamitously died at only one year old from meningitis. On being told that Freda must be admitted to Gulson Road Hospital Grace tearfully cried out 'Oh no, not the workhouse!' Gulson Road Hospital had been until 1929 the infirmary of Coventry workhouse and bad memories linger in an oppressed population.

Coventry and Warwickshire was the local hospital as far as mother was concerned and she had taken part in the money raising carnival and Godiva procession to raise money for its upkeep, dressed as a jester but gave up on it when the money raised was no longer used to sustain the hospital. Mother often repeated that Freda died of 'cerebrospinal spotted fever' and doctors had tried an experimental serum, as a last resort, so that she died with needle holes all over her head. The death certificate confirms meningitis.

The tragedy was compounded when the next born, Walter, also died in infancy at just two years old. The family never truly recovered from these deaths and they overshadowed my own young life. It's no surprise that Mum was traumatised by it all, her distress increased by the attitude adopted by Dad's family on Freda's death.

Unfortunately the house was shared with Dad's sister Win her husband Jim and children Alan and Rose and after Freda died Gran and Win trailed all over the house carrying burning coals on a shovel in the mistaken belief that this would drive out noxious organisms, entering the rooms occupied by my parent's. Dad being at work Mum had to face this alone and although the act was not necessarily unkind but merely foolish it showed a complete lack of empathy and discretion to choose a time when a mother who'd just suffered the death of her one year old was without the support of her husband. She never forgave them.

Mum had problems with their interference on many occasions which culminated in Gran being ejected from my parent's room which she'd insisted on entering. Dad intercepted her at the door, as Mum used to tell with satisfaction, and 'Put his hand on her face and backed her out of the room'. The feuding and nit-picking criticism around the family in general and that aimed at Gran by my mother in particular at first upset and later exasperated me.

After the death of Freda the family moved to 210 Sewell Highway, I assume the relationship between Aunt Win and Mum was partly to blame; Mum always regretted leaving Church Lane and would sigh and point out the house whenever we were passing. I had always assumed the death of Walter took place while the family lived there but on acquiring a copy of the death certificate learned that they had already moved house.

This fact changed my perception of the family home I was born into, I'd believed for over sixty years that my parents had moved to 210 after the death of both infants and made a fresh start. That the brother I never knew experienced the house and garden, was taken out in his push chair for walks and to the Co-op, all the things that I thought were unique to me in that house, and in addition knew the Dump when it was only a field at the bottom of the garden, subtly disordered my memories of my old family home.

Mum said that Walter had been ill but seemed to have recovered and that he and she were in the front garden when he suddenly 'messed himself' said 'I'm sorry Mammy' and that his eyes rolled back in his head as he lost consciousness. These were his last words and later he died.

On acquiring a copy of his death certificate as part of my research for this book I realised that my assumption of another sibling death due to meningitis was wrong, the cause of death came as a shock, subarachnoid haemorrhage.

The story I was told is that Syd and Walter both grabbed hold of one of the items on the fireplace companion set, they both tugged hard, Syd let go and the implement whacked Walter on the head and this was blamed for the death. Syd was eight years and Walter two, it seemed unlikely that a two year old tugging anything from his brother's hand would exert enough force and I had thought of this explanation as a fanciful rejection by Mum of meningitis once more taking her offspring. Once the cause of death became known to me it became probable that Walter too had haemophilia. Mild to moderate trauma may have initiated bleeding, another possibility, as I recall that Mum told me he'd been ill but had recovered, together with a vague memory that he'd been hospitalised at that time, is that of previous intracranial infection precipitating later bleeding. On being asked by me the specifics of Walter's death Mum replied 'I don't know something to do with his brain.' An unsatisfactory answer but to have probed further would have been unkind.

After Walter's death Syd went to live with our grandparents for a while. Mum never spoke of it but someone told me, when I was much too young to process the information, that she blamed Syd for the death of both siblings but whether this put Syd in physical danger I doubt, the rejection couldn't have done him much good psychologically that's certain if the story is true. I suspect, or perhaps hope, that compassion may have played a part in his removal as I imagine Mum was in a bad state on the death of a second child and needed time to recover.

It was true that in my mother's eyes Syd was the cause of the death of both infant son and daughter.

Freda had caught meningitis after she and Syd were taken to a fairground sitting opposite each other in a pram. Many soldiers on leave were part of the crowd and the doctors suggested that these had brought the disease in but Syd had vomited on his sister and this Mum believed was the cause of the disease that carried her off.

I don't suppose this was a belief shared by Syd. On the other hand he once, chillingly, told me that he had killed his little brother.

Chapter 6

That he was responsible for his brother's death he had fully accepted although a slight blow as a cause of death seemed unlikely to me and in retrospect I should have asked him to elaborate but as the confession was quite sudden, apropos nothing as I recall, I was too shaken and perhaps too young to know what to say. He didn't offer to elaborate either at the time or thereafter and I never raised the subject at a later date remembering how he'd looked away from me as he said it then walked. I think he decided he'd said enough. It is of course possible that there was a little more to the episode than an accident but I firmly believe haemophilia to have been the real culprit. What a cruel burden for him to carry.

Eighteen months after Walter's death came the formality of a declaration of war and World War 2 began. That the next few years were full of fear, privation and mourning in the family and within the city is a given but also apparent is that saturation bombing destroying homes, businesses and lives brought out the best in those under attack. Bravery of many kinds, compassion, and ingenuity were needed as rationing of food and clothing and the scarcity of many other goods added to the terror bombing ensured mutual support was necessary for survival. Not that it was all sweet harmony, a black market in rationed goods quickly developed and in some places petty opportunistic theft was rife, not to say looting. Syd was evacuated out of the bombing, as were so many, in his case to relatives at Hinckley and Mum and Dad tried to carry on as usual which meant a greater struggle to survive and the resourceful use of every opportunity. They took to keeping hens as Dad had done as a boy thus providing eggs for the family while the surplus was bartered for other essentials, maximising what could be obtained during rationing.

The only memory of his sojourn in Hinckley that Syd ever mentioned was a fight with a cousin when on the boy saying he needed a job he suggested a paper round not realising 'job'' was the local idiom for defecation. Who won he didn't say!

Gerry Northern was a mate acquired at special school but who lived only a couple of streets away from my home and it seems strange that we never met at the local shops or bus terminus. I can be certain that the prejudice and fear of association felt by other kids in the neighbourhood had no part to play; I'd simply not met him. Gerry was ostracised and at times ridiculed by the gormless element because of his cerebral palsy. I'd had the luck to spend time around many with disabilities or chronic illnesses, feeling no fear or superiority but admiration for the strength it took to live among the ignorant or patronising. Thankfully Gerry's speech was not a problem and he could walk albeit unsteadily but his chief problem was manual dexterity, spasms when handling small objects making life difficult at times. If walking is truthfully said to be controlled falling forward then to watch Gerry walk was to witness an exaggerated performance of the act. He did very well in fact however precarious his progress seemed although a minor trip or sudden jostle could see him down on the ground if his attempt to grab me for support was foiled as I shrugged him off. When he succeeded he would have me over too when my only expedient was to arrange for him to cushion my fall by landing on top.

He claimed to have friends in the area although I never saw him with anyone except others of our gang and the only time I saw him interact with boys unknown to me was when a bunch were playing football and he went over and, with assumed nonchalance asked: Any chance of a game? He was told no, he couldn't play football anyway and he responded that he played for the Red Rovers. One of them replied: You mean the Red-Arsed Rovers, Fuck off Gerry! He shrugged and the pair of us acceded to the yob's crude advice.

Never one to consider the consequences of his actions, at school, in a rural science lesson arranged for participant refugees from several classes, incidentally extremely interesting to me and so short – lived, on hearing Mrs. Burt use the word manure he interrupted with 'poo' and was rebuked but on the spreading of the soil conditioner getting its mention he again said 'poo' and on being told to leave the room 'poo' and on closing the door behind him 'poo'.

Gerry could be very foolish whenever the fancy took him and in the end this led to banning from our street club after two ridiculous incidents. The first when for a reason unknown he threw earth and dry leaves onto the side of newly painted van belonging to a neighbour, for which he received a warning and the second an act of vandalism right under the nose of a building site watchman claiming I'd told him to. He still came around, there was no ostracism he just wasn't welcome in the club or privy to its nefarious doings. He was only teased once, bullied would be too harsh a term. He required a private moment with the bathroom porcelain and as the gang were busy surveying a building site for mischief a workman's latrine, a wooden hut over a pit, was recommended and once inside we fixed the door trapping him. The trick was not prolonged and after his first screech for help we let him out.

He never bore a grudge for long even after sitting in a wash basin, one of a row in the school toilet block when I'd pushed him away as he'd tried to intimidate me. He landed in the sink and the whole row of them which were joined together came away from the wall all the waste pipes bending together to lower him gently to the floor from where scrambling to his feet he told me to look what I'd done. I instructed him to lift one end while I did the same at the other and we straightened the row until it was impossible to tell its recent history.

There was no way he could blame me for further incidents, in particular his enduring intimate contact with a stand of stinging nettles. On The Dump, our waste land adventure playground he tripped made a wild grab for me, missed and landed flat on his back amongst the nettles. On being stung he started to yell and demand that I help him up, I declined as I knew the chances of him pulling me down putting us both in difficulties were very high. I told him he'd have to roll over and stand up, he complained he'd be stung more and I replied he should just get on, do it and be done. He complied and I took him to my home where Mum dabbed his throbbing hands and face with a blue-bag an archaic laundry aid renowned as a sure-fire cure for the irritation of stings. Off Gerry went his face and hands liberally dotted with blue spots, still he was used to being stared at.

His never failing interest in football and our recent acquisition of a television, which his family didn't possess, led to Gerry and his father being invited round to watch the cup final. Drinks were proffered and in his excitement he bit a piece out of his glass of lemonade. He wasn't cut and his attention never wavered from the screen even when Mum took the glass and told him not to worry and although his father apologised Gerry didn't appear to notice there had been a minor crisis. I was to meet his father only twice more.

Mr Northern came to see Dad unexpectedly; he had a proposal to make that Gerry and I should go into business together, presumably with a little financial assistance from Dad. At school we had a small printing press and Gerry had taken to printing in a big way. His parents bought a small press and all that was needed and the idea was that Gerry would use his printing knowledge and skills to support himself. The printing system at the time involved setting up small metal letters to make up the words an essential part of the job Gerry could not manage because of the manual dexterity issue so his parents would do that part to his instructions. Obviously this situation could not be expected to last and equally obviously the gentle nature of the job would suit me as a haemophiliac. I'd not been consulted and although the thinking behind the scheme was good I'm not sure it would have worked or that it was what I wanted. In the event it didn't matter what my opinion would have been because I wasn't asked and Dad immediately turned the suggestion down.

For a number of years Gerry travelled around on a tricycle taking orders for headed note paper and envelopes the printing done by him and his parents, how profitable this was and if it provided a living I can't say, as we lost touch. Shortly before this I accompanied him and his parents to a local pub where he told me that some silly man at one of the tables was going to put a word in for him and get him a job in one of the car factories, and why didn't I buy the man a drink and he would do the same for me. Oh dear, poor Gerry, I wasn't going to be taken in and yes of course nothing in the form of a job came his way, the usual fruit of drunken and stupid patronage.

The inevitable happened, his parents died and he moved away to Leeds where the family originated to live with relatives. Some years back he must have made a visit to Coventry because I saw him almost at the top of an escalator in a local city centre store. Two middle-aged women behind him were mocking him by moving their heads unsteadily. I didn't call to him or shout at them as I was afraid of startling him and causing an accident, so I rushed for the lift but in spite of a store wide search couldn't find him. That glimpse was never repeated.

My father was born in Coventry in 1905, one of three children; Winifred the eldest, and Robert who in later life he would quarrel with and thereafter never speak to again, the youngest. Due to his reiteration of many of his life episodes I have retained more of his memories of childhood than of my mother's.

As a boy he got into many a scrape and he told me all about them and his games and pranks.

Chapter 7

Today he and his mates would find themselves beset by social workers and other misguided individuals of the caring type and police warnings or become saddled with anti-social behaviour orders but back then those caught in the act would be punished and those that got away with it merely cursed. Vandalism of a mild and creative nature would cover most 'crimes' or petty theft.

Theft first, Dad and his mates would each take a length of timber and drive a nail through one end then charge down the local shopping street, Ball Hill, past the greengrocer's and smack down on the goods displayed outside. 'You might be lucky and get a couple of bananas, an apple or orange or be unlucky and gain a turnip or cabbage.' They would keep on running and it was over so quickly they were never caught. Attempted fraud rather than outright theft he accomplished in solitary.

Boys made a little pocket money selling match day programmes outside Coventry City's ground, and were given a number to sell at a penny each and on returning to the man who had the concession the pennies were stacked up into shillings, twelve to a pile, the sellers were paid one penny for every pile of twelve. Dad tried the job once. Very soon, being venturesome, he hit on an idea that would maximise his 'wages' and set out his takings in piles of eleven instead; this appeared to be working as the proprietor, with a dab of his finger counted the stacks, unfortunately a third of the way through he stopped, picked one up and counted only eleven pennies. Dad was rewarded for his capitalist venture by soundly boxed ears and left with nothing except the instruction never to show his face again.

On a day when fun was lagging behind the time to enjoy it they would run down the greengrocer's street past the ironmongers, where all kinds of gardening tools would be hanging outside for sale and sticking out their hands as they ran knock them all over the pavement. Once more they would keep on running. The ironmonger got his revenge however and on the last occasion they carried out this minor offence he had tapped into the handles of the implements tin-tacks, as a consequence when they dragged their hands along the line their fingers suffered many jagged cuts which could not be explained to parents for fear of a beating.

In streets where the terraced house front door led straight on to the pavement, two adjacent door knockers would be tied loosely together with rope and both doors knocked. When two householders opened their respective doors the fun was immense as both the targeted tugged and pulled, yelled and sometimes cursed whoever they thought was pulling on the other side of the door. Another way to plague the neighbours involved pushing a drawing pin into the window frame of a curtained window, a coat button would be tied to the end of a reel of black thread and dangled just above the window when the boys would hide around the corner and lower the button then jiggle it until it tap-tapped and then haul it up out of sight. The victim would pull the curtain wide enough to peer out, and seeing nothing and no – one would let the curtain close. After a minute or so the procedure would resume and increasingly irritated the victim would again pull open the curtains, taking an even closer look into the street and on the third or fourth tapping would emerge, take a long look up and down the street and go back indoors to immediately hear tap, tap, tap again when he would fling open the door and charge out glaring and muttering. As the trick took place only after dark gloom concealed the black thread and button.

Street gangs we hear so often, from those for whom history is bunk, are terrible modern phenomena but my generation had them, we called them clubs and my father and his set were certainly a gang. These gangs were very local in membership, usually drawn from only a few streets and were bad luck to an unwary stranger. Fights were commonplace but a newcomer to the area if he escaped physical challenge faced all kinds of tricks.

Wild Horse Kick Back was a game that had the advantage of annoying a neighbour and punishing a trespasser or interloper in the gang's territory. The unsuspecting dupe would be asked if he wanted a game and told he was to be blindfolded and put with his back to a fence when the others would chant 'wild horse kick back, kick back, kick back while they hid and when he no longer heard them he was to take off the blindfold and seek them out. In fact he had been placed with his back to someone's front door and would find himself smacked around the head and told to 'clear off'.

It was not always possible to evade authority and an incident concerning a large plate glass window, still there many years later fronting a grocery shop in Clay Lane, meant a brush with the law. The window had a small hole in the glass, which must have been exceptionally strong, where an airgun pellet or stone from a catapult had hit, the rest of this glass not even cracked and consequently not worth the considerable cost of replacing. Behind the glass the grocer had placed a tempting bowl of eggs. The temptation proved too strong and requiring his mates to wait he rushed home to arrive back with a knitting needle with which he attempted to spear the eggs through the hole. The operation was difficult as the needle kept sliding off the seemingly armour-plated eggshells but with his fascinated mates standing behind watching diligence and perseverance paid off, as we're often told they must, and he turned, his face lit with triumph. 'Got it!' to find himself alone apart from looming over him a police constable who smacked him round the head with his gloves then took him home for the usual punishment.

Only once were he and his cronies, when a little older, actually chased by the police when they escaped capture by running in at the back and out at the front door of a conveniently placed house just after the family sat down to eat, thankfully they remembered their manners.

As each boy went crashing past the dining table he politely gasped: Good evening Mrs Brown, good evening Mr Brown!

These and many more were the innocent pursuits indulged in by (some of!) our fathers in those long gone days of civility and decorum when children were seen and not heard. I know that your sensibilities would be indelibly besmirched by other revelations of a more lavatorial nature so will leave them alone. Come on now, you don't really wish to know about the more disgusting tricks? You do! Well thanks for twisting my arm. Briefly then.

'More in it' required the stock unwary stranger and his cap. Advised to leave his cap on the ground he would be blindfolded and told to chant 'more in it' and wait for a surprise. Once he became bored and suspicious of the subdued tittering he would snatch off the blindfold to find someone peeing into his already sodden cap.

'Hold my stick!' Two boys jostle while others watch, the victim, approaching, senses a fight. A boy holding a stick says to the new kid: Here kid, hold my stick while I see to him. The victim grabs the end of the proffered stick which is then pulled through his hand. The end of the stick was sticky with faeces now the hand is instead.

The other excremental trick concerned a similar sap, an old cap and doggy crap. Cap over crap, kneeling boys reluctant to retrieve what is under cap, sap says 'What is it, a bird? I'll get it! He's obviously eager to be accepted by his new-found chums as the unafraid newcomer. He pulls out the faecal 'bird'' eliciting only sneering contempt and laughter.

Dad's sister Win doesn't feature a great deal in these pages, she died shortly before I was born so I have no direct memory of her but two incidents concerning their games were told to me by Dad.

Brother and sister were playing hide and seek in the street, Win finding an excellent hiding place as she could not be found. The road sweeper, who had been elsewhere and had left his cart unattended suddenly strode up and pushed it into motion. One of the two lids flew up and out popped the head and shoulders of a screaming Win, the poor man screamed too and buckled at the knees. Gran came running and later Dad was chastised for Win's escapade.

He also found himself on the receiving end of a 'tanning' after a more reprehensible episode involving Win as his partner in crime; how he thought of it and how he could believe that getting away with it was a possibility I have no idea. The baker used to deliver bread from his horse – drawn van and the pair of them greeted his day's effort in their street by shouting 'Baker, baker, shit a cold tater'. Whether this charming advisory phrase was common currency at the time, specific to the trade of baker or not, or merely of his own devising is a mystery. The upshot was that Dad was severely beaten for the impudence, the language and for leading his sister into disreputable, unladylike behaviour.

A horse and another odd-toed ungulate, that is a donkey, both earned a mention in my father's memories of his well spent youth.

Chapter 8

On one of those days when the horrors of school had been escaped a number of the gang went to the city centre looking for mischief. In one or other of the old cobbled streets, sadly destroyed by Nazi bombs but at the time quaintly mediaeval, a horse harnessed to a dray loaded with empty casks was quietly standing outside a public house waiting for the boss while he, no doubt, sampled the newly arrived ale. Out of a wretches' pocket came a catapult and saying 'watch this' he shot a marble which in Dad's words 'hit it straight on the dick'. The startled animal reared up between the shafts and bolted down the narrow street, casks broke free and bowled alongside and the dray turned over and smashed against a wall. No bystander suffered injury although they might well have and the horse, one sore and swollen place apart, came to no harm. The consensus of opinion was that the usually docile animal had been stung by an insect. No repercussions ensued for the culprits.

The donkey, Neddy as tradition demanded, and his driver were well known in the city and here I'll state that this donkey was a paragon as to patience, being required to wait for its proprietor outside many a hostelry for many an hour whilst the business of imbibing liquor titillated the reprobate palate. On noticing this regular phenomenon the boys disrobed Neddy of his harness, tipped the cart on its side and carried it through the archway into the pub's yard, righted it and re-attached Neddy. They tested their own patience and waited until the fully topped up and staggering driver emerged. 'What the hell, are you doing in there Ned? Come on.' And he tried to lead Neddy out. The cart, being too wide, couldn't pass through the archway and after scratching his head he went back into the pub and brought out landlord and cronies to marvel at Neddy's magic. Dad and his cronies made off before common sense and sobriety, if any were sober, suggested the obvious answer.

He would often chuckle and recount how he returned home from school, after his first day, carrying his soiled shorts over his shoulders by the braces. I often speculate whether the loose bowels could have announced the onset of the illness, the memory of which terrified him for the rest of his life, the fever. Which fever I never asked and he never volunteered scarlet, typhoid, or something else? I do know he was desperately ill and had a very high temperature and never forgot the hallucinations suffered. 'You wouldn't want to see the things I saw when I had the fever'. Pressed as to detail he would only repeat himself and that is all he would say.

Like most adventurous boys he sometimes found himself a victim of his own making as when his head became, in classic fashion, trapped between railings; easy to stick through but impossible to pull it back, he was trapped for some time, and in tears when in his words: A big buck navvy came along, put his knee on one upright, both hands on the other, pulled and spread them apart saying 'Why, you silly little bugger!'

Window cleaners, when Dad was a boy, used a two wheeled handcart to carry ladders and other tools of the trade and this when unattended made a good slide, climb to the front and slide down. Unfortunately there happened to be a couple of hooks for the buckets and Dad became impaled on one of them, the hook penetrating his shorts and the cheek of his backside and there he hung until released by someone carefully removing him against the curve of the hook, leaving two neat entry and exit wounds. A few inches lower and I might not have been here to write this.

Another narrow escape happened when he disobeyed his parents and went to watch the rioting which has always been a feature of my home city throughout history. While feeling sorry for the horses I admired the innovation with which they and their police riders were met with buckets of ball bearings discharged into the road and the ensuing chaos of slipping, sliding, and falling. Later the crowd surged back under renewed police violence and Dad was crushed against a door which suddenly opened and a hand roughly dragged him inside where he was clipped round the ear and let out the back way with instructions to run home. Which of the many riots indulged in by the citizens of Coventry I can't now recall being told, it seems unlikely that the 1919 well documented rioting over three days was referred to as the impression I got was of a younger child but I could be wrong of course.

One story told of his going to see the first aeroplane to land in the city and how a large crowd gathered to await the landing and greet the pilot. Excitement zipped through them as the plane taxied to a standstill and the crowd, including my father, rushed forward, the last action of one poor soul who, not realising the danger, was decapitated. The head bounced and rolled like a football and someone left the stunned crowd as understanding of the tragedy hit home and dropped a coat over the remains. The deflated crowd, after a number of horrified screams, silently looked on.

The landing could well have been in 1916 on Hearsall Common, though my memory is that Dad said Whitley, if so then he would have been aged eleven years and Frank Whittle, who history tells us was also there, nine years.

Dad was nine years old at the beginning of the 1914-18 world war and shared his recollections with me.

The fevered height of anti -German feeling may be gauged from the thwarted attack on the home of a doctor who lived in a large house next to Primrose Hill Park. The doctor had been much respected before the war, but had a German sounding name and was thus suspected, by the inflamed ignorant, of being a spy. The mob had to be restrained by the police and my father never failed to point out the house every time we passed it.

Another incident made a big impression on me when told of it and an even bigger impression on my father at the time. He was in the city centre with my granddad where the labour of German prisoners of war, under guard, was being utilised in some way, when a drunken idiot emerged from one of the numerous pubs and began verbally abusing them and raising his fist to one of the prisoners was about to strike when the soldier guarding them leapt forward, with fixed bayonet.

Forcing the drunkard back against the wall he told him: Keep your hands to yourself, I won't hesitate to stick you like a pig. If you want to fight get out to where this one's been and go through what he's been through. There spoke a soldier even I would have been proud to know although I acknowledge few heroes. One other hero from his memories of childhood was the woman, a teacher, who refused to lead her class in saluting the flag on Empire Day. Needless to say she was dismissed.

One prank earned Dad kudos amongst his contemporaries and amused tolerance from his elders. He rigged up a mock telegraph system from his bedroom to a large tree next to the house and down to ground level, a surreptitious yank on the cable would set an alarm clock ringing when he would tell the credulous that he had another message coming in, run up to his bedroom and the alarm silenced, emerge and tell them, when asked, that he was not allowed to reveal the content.

His fun came to an end when the tree's roots became a danger to the house's foundations and although a useful and elegant walnut it had to go. The task was given to Dad who approached the job like a professional, cutting from the top and lowering each piece to the ground, earning a shilling from the landlord's agent Mr Reeve who was startled to be informed by Gran that he owed her son a fee with the puzzling information 'Oh, Mr Reeve there's a shilling up your sleeve.' The poor man desperately searched both sleeves bleating 'Where, where?' until realisation and more reasonable information led him to hand over the shilling.

Bonfire night, the fifth of November, was celebrated with vigour and, as in my own childhood, very often to the consternation of neighbours.

Dad and a few of his mates stood in a covered entry between terraced houses – these produced wonderful reverberating echoes – and banged a large baulk of timber up and down on the paving, chanting 'Please to remember, the fifth of November gunpowder, treason and plot.' If their efforts could be called a 'plot' then it proved as bad an idea as Mr Fawkes' had, the heavy vibration caused decorative plates to come crashing down on the inside of one of the two houses separated by the entry and the furious householder rushed out hitting them around the head with a walking stick! No assault charges in those long gone days, if they'd complained to their parents they would have received further punishment.

When older they caused a marvellous explosion as one of the older boys had a job metal-turning and produced a tube with a screw cap and small hole for a fuse. Naturally they filled it with black- powder, added a fuse, placed it and struck a match, fortunately they had the sense enough to stand well back, where they were gratified by the explosion but astonished by the resultant damage as a large section of the wall against which the device had stood was demolished. They made off before unpleasant consequences accrued.

I learnt reinforcing lessons from these two November tales.

Chapter 9

From the latter, explosives can be fun but may have unforeseen consequences, and from both incidents, you can't be caught if you're not around to reap what you have sown. Yes folks, don't get caught!

Apart from the typical pursuits of a street urchin he had various hobbies and pastimes which he entered into with his usual enthusiasm. He kept fowl, both laying hens and bantams, the experience of which came in useful during the Second World War. On first introducing a bantam cock into the run, as all the fowl were kept together, he was warned that the resident full-sized cockerel would kill the bantam. He told his adviser to watch and sure enough the bantam when challenged hopped onto the back of the larger bird and crowed, thereafter becoming king of the roost. I think this story pleased him in the telling because of his not being exactly tall and his own tenacious will to win. Also of great significance to him was that The Bantams was then the nickname of his beloved Coventry City F C.

The team started life as works club, Singer F C and played on land close to Britannia Street at some point in their early history, Dad often reiterated to me that the building at the back of the Binley Oak pub, which in my early manhood was the home of Coventry Folk Club, had once been the football club's dressing room. He regretted the passing of the days when football fans amused themselves before the match by chucking old hats behind the goal if Luton town were the opponents or kippers if a 'seaside' team formed the opposition, and a city fan – not my father – would release a bantam cock onto the pitch and catch it up just before kick-off, a good result forecast if it crowed in the meantime!

A source of family income that he accessed during hard times as a boy was the prize money to be had at fetes and other gatherings where his speed over the ground, possibly nurtured by being required to run away from the trouble he'd caused, enabled him to win. Half-a-crown, twelve and a half pence in today's money was a regular acquisition and once or twice five shillings a veritable fortune for a boy. Prize money was always handed over to his mother and a few pennies given back to him to spend.

Running and dribbling a ball were skills that must have been very useful when playing for the football team managed by an uncle. The team was named after the house where either he or his uncle lived, my memory is unclear on the point although I have a photograph of him as a young child sitting outside the house and someone has reddened the name over the door which read Rose Villa. An active wiry lad, strong and sharp but not tall he was offered a place at a horse racing stables where he would have ridden horses to work and might have one day made it as a jockey. This would have meant living away and his parents said no. Whenever he told me this story a measure of wistful regret would be evident.

The collecting of wild bird's eggs was not looked at as despicable when he was a boy as with fewer pressures on wildlife than today, when a great many birds are in decline, was in skilful hands not as detrimental. He and his mates were avid collectors, walking miles into the countryside looking for nests, only one egg being taken from each found and great care taken not to cause damage to the nest or vegetation. One of their favourite areas was Whitley which, at that time, was the home of the sewage works. As he eloquently put it 'Eric Waterman fell into the shit tank and chased us all the way home crying and begging us to stop but we ran all the harder to keep away from him.' This may seem unfeeling, even cruel but my father and, I imagine most others were afraid of catching something let alone the awful smell; Dad with his memory of 'the fever' and running prowess probably led the way.

When Eric reached home his mother made him undress in the garden, where his clothes were later burnt, and pour buckets of water over himself washing with carbolic soap.

My grandparents rented several different houses over the years, 23 Craner's Road, 61 Smith Street off Red Lane where he was born, Payne's Lane, Mulliner Street and lastly 154 Villiers Street. There may have been more but I recall only those. Of Payne's Lane he told me only this memory.

As a man he was not the sort to have a belief in the supernatural but an incident occurred which was never explained to his satisfaction.

One night the family had made their way to bed but were not yet asleep when the sound of the front door opening was heard and footsteps on the stairs, but the most frightening aspect was the unmistakeable sound of a hand running up the wall as someone, or something, ascended. Grandad leapt out of bed and rushed to the top of the stairs brandishing a walking stick with the rest of the family behind him but there was no one there. The sounds suddenly stopped and when the house was searched the doors, back and front, remained locked and bolted and everything was in order and in its accustomed place. The experience was never repeated and no explanation ever found.

In one of the rooms there was the outline of some kind of hatch or cupboard behind wallpaper and he'd never been comfortable with it and after the above 'ghostly' intervention never allowed himself to be on his own there.

From several sources including my research into family history I have been able to learn substantially more about my father's parents, grandparents and great grandparents than my mother's.

His maternal grandfather, John Wood had worked with horses for most of his working life until forced to move to the city when his job as farm bailiff in north Warwickshire came to an end on one of the periodic downturns in agricultural affairs. He found employment as a gardener at St. Joseph's Convent established in 1868 and sited opposite historical Gosford Green, venue of a past royal led anti-climax – which I will not go into here – which was later destroyed by wartime bombing. Dad was put off gardening, being obliged to help him plant out row on row of cabbage plants. Great-Grandad Wood was getting on in years and as a gardener was feeling his age so decided he needed the help of up-to-date equipment. Pushing a wheelbarrow with a wooden wheel and iron rimmed tyre over wet and heavy ground was becoming all too strenuous an activity for him and he remarked to, I imagine, the amusement of the listeners, that he needed 'One of them new fangled barrers with a rheumatic tyre'.

His knowledge of working horses was encyclopaedic and it's certain he would have taken a very dim view of his grandson's catapult exploit. What this preamble is leading to is that on business in the city centre he stopped and examined the forelegs of a dray horse, when out of a pub (yes, yet another pub) came the driver to be met with a shout of 'Young man, you've had this horse down on his shammocks, you ought to be ashamed of yourself. Let me catch you again and you'll get some of this.' This was his walking stick which he was waving in the young man's face. The inference behind 'down on his shammocks' was that the cart had been overloaded and the poor animal had been forced, probably whipped, down onto its knees, injuring them, in order to gain forward motion.

John Wood was a typical countryman whose family, for as far back as I have been able to trace, had lived in and around the village of Baddesley Ensor, north

Warwickshire for generations and while bailiff at Lower House Farm he had patented a ploughshare adapted to the particular soil conditions, such local adaptations often being patented, and I'm afraid this brought nothing but derision from my father as did the employment as farm bailiff. Dad used to scoff and tell me a bailiff was nothing more than a foreman! If John Wood been around to hear this I'm sure it would have elicited his usual angry cry of 'Damn me saints!'

Of his grandmother Wood, Caroline, Dad only spoke once to tell me of the insults that passed between the old couple. She would call John an 'ole reprobate' and he would call her a 'fornicating crow'. It's a certainty that he couldn't have told you what fornicating meant, apart from it being frowned upon in the Bible, but crows he would have shot on a good many occasions. His daughter, my paternal grandmother had, in a glass case, stuffed and mounted, a bird rarely seen in Britain; a hoopoe which had unwisely chosen to perch on top of the local church steeple, no doubt seeking sanctuary and had been shot by another of the Woods as something out of the ordinary, a fate not unusual where ignorance perceives difference.

The Haughtons I have traced back to my great-great-grandfather, Frederick William born 1818 in London, St. Pancras. Frederick was recorded as being a station master living in Durham in the 1851 census and in those subsequent as, variously, clerk, gaol officer, bailiff in legal possession of a farm and schoolmaster in 1871 when his wife Eliza was recorded as schoolmistress.

On a genealogy site someone researching the Haughtons holds the belief that the pair served as staff members at a workhouse but on scrutinising the minute books of both the Coventry Union and Foleshill Union I find no mention of them any capacity.

Prior to the Poor Law Amendment Act of 1834 work houses existed but were less punishing and uncomfortable, the poor looked on as persons who through circumstance had fallen on hard times. A whole mass (mess) of legislation dating back to the 1600's concerning relief of poverty had resulted in a regime Spartan but not institutionally harsh. In 1834 this changed to a belief that poverty was the fault of the poor themselves and that they must be discouraged from seeking help.

Chapter 10

The act was passed though not entirely without opponents including William Cobbett, the campaign against continuing with boycotts and disruptive demonstrations outside meetings of boards of guardians until Joseph Rayner Stephens was found guilty of sedition and inflammatory speeches and imprisoned.

The new act required each parish to elect a board of guardians whose duty was to oversee the workhouse, collect the poor rate from householders and report to the commissioners. Smaller parishes joined together as Unions.

All those seeking relief were to be taken in to the workhouse, no more 'outdoor relief' to alleviate poverty by the provision of money, food or goods, men women and children were segregated and if fit put to work. The pre 1834 regime had been based on the principle of 'The poor are always with us.' but the nature of Christian charity now on display may be gauged from the historical account of a workhouse master complaining of a 'lunatic' who could only be controlled by beating around the head and toes with a stick.

Coventry prior to the act had several 'houses of industry' which finally ceased to exist after 1834 as far as I can tell. Thereafter Coventry Union and Foleshill Union were responsible for the city's resident poor. Both Unions took in disabled and elderly infirm poor people. How in 1881 the Coventry Union's one recorded lunatic was treated is not documented in the list of inmates. No physical disabilities are mentioned apart from one blind man so it seems likely that the thirteen imbeciles included cases of severe CP or other disabilities where communication was difficult or absent. I have read of an inmate of a workhouse elsewhere who was recorded as an imbecile in a document and in a census as 'Deaf and Dumb'.

In Dickens' Oliver Twist we see the worst of the system but the administration of the Unions depended on the parishes' means and the Guardians competence and empathy. He wrote of a workhouse in his periodical 'All The Year Round': I had knocked at the gate of the workhouse of St. George's-in-the-East, and had found it to be an establishment highly creditable to those parts, and thoroughly well administered by a most intelligent master. This suggests that Dickens was not highly critical of the system itself but the calibre of those overseeing it.

Joseph my great-grandfather was born during the time Frederick and Eliza lived in Durham. Frederick, station master according to the 1851 census, possibly for the North Eastern Railway was tried for embezzlement, the white-collar crime tending to confirm his status, thankfully he was found not guilty. Subsequently the family moved to Coventry but also lived for a time in Birmingham before returning again to Coventry.

Joseph after working at a tannery in Kenilworth is recorded in various documents as a watchmaker. Dad re-told the story that his grandfather, Joseph, would come into the workshop and if those working for him had run short of gold he would take out two or three sovereigns and drop them into the melting pot. Does this, if accurate, mean that the business was involved in case making rather than watch escapements or dials? Components were made in separate establishments and assembled thereafter. I have been unable to confirm Joseph as a watchmaker.

Joseph married Alice Prudence Mather in 1877 but died aged only forty-one just sixteen years later. Alice kept a sweet shop for a time and is registered as a confectioners assistant in the 1901 census but by 1911 a midwife, ten years is long enough for even such change I suppose but the details of how this was accomplished are a mystery to me. Was she in fact only an assistant confectioner or perhaps she progressed to own the business? Anyway, the business failed this I do know; Dad told me it was because she gave too many sweets away to the raggedy urchins with their noses pressed up against the shop window, eyes wide and mouths watering and vice versa, she couldn't resist.

Joseph's business also failed because of too strong a liking for alcohol; he would be brought home in a horse drawn cab at all hours after, presumably, sovereigns the like of which he once threw into the melting pot were now bunged into the coffers of a pub landlord. Alice survived him until 1937 dying in her eightieth year. As a midwife she served the community of Hillfields and Foleshill and would often be called out in the night to assist women on boats at the canal basin, where her father had been a coal porter.

Walter Frederick, Joseph and Alice's son and my paternal grandfather married Rose Hannah Wood and they had three children, Winifred, Sydney and Robert.

My grandparent's house in Villiers Street, Stoke Coventry was one of a terraced row whose front – doors opened directly onto the street from what we knew as the front room which akin to many such rooms was rarely used, the air striking cold, and the fire place usually devoid of fire. At the window an aspidistra and a scented leaved pelargonium and placed on the carpet two curious mats made from long strips of coloured felt woven and stitched together but the most fascinating object was a stuffed bird in its glass case, rewarded for its journeying, by an executioner from Gran's family.

Anyone showing an interest would be admonished not to touch as the slightest vibration could cause it to disintegrate so permanency was guaranteed; it could not be moved! Oh ye of little faith in the ways of taxidermy! Several surreptitious gentle raps and shoves convinced me that its frailty was a fiction.

A chaise longue I recall, on which I was obliged to lie one day with a teaspoonful of whisky held in my cheek to deaden the pain of toothache. Gran's treatment worked only as long as the whisky remained around the tooth and the alcohol slipping down the throat on an involuntary swallow, the pain soon returned and required another spoonful. This could not go on for long of course but by the third application much less pain was evident.

In the back yard, next to the WC was a construction made of old bricks stuccoed with a concrete mix which had fallen off in places. Some kind of plant, reduced to brittle twigs grew out of the earth with which it was filled and a shrunken fern hung onto life with tenacity equal to my own. This carbuncle or excrescence, referred to as The Grotto, clung to, or seemed to well out of the fabric of the building and everyone passed it by without a second look, everyone but me. I was equally bemused by the opposite wall upon which someone with a strange sense of irony had nailed quietly rotting strips of cloth similar to those used to make rag-rugs, there was no pattern to this phenomenon and I didn't like to ask the function or alternatively the reasoning behind this manifestation of my grandparent's endeavour. Not until my teens did I realise that there must have been in the long gone, a climbing plant against the wall supported by the nail and cloth strip technique!

Next door lived a witch. Mrs Forrester was, like many poor old widows persecuted in the past, just that, a poor old woman all alone and whether she knew anything of the use of medicinal herbs, a terrible crime when Christianity ruled, was not an issue. For me as a child she was a witch.

I must, when very young,have ventured into her yard for I have a strong memory of seeing her sitting in a chair, dressed all in black, thin faced, nose and chin gravitating toward a common point, the chair set on a floor covered with torn up paper and other rubbish.

I would see her peering and scowling out of the window every time I passed her yard on visiting Gran and Grandad. Just her head and shoulders that's how I know my seeing her in a chair in the midst of disgusting chaos happened when I was an intrepid toddler. Her face, lined and grimy, remains fixed in my mind though how I can know it was grimy is another mystery. I found her menacing but the stare that unnerved me may only have been that of someone whose eyes were failing.

The back of the house was reached through an entry between two of the houses, narrower than the entries back home it was in fact a tunnel as the upstairs portion of the houses on either side roofed it in. It was echoey and footsteps rang strangely with shouting frowned upon though I suppose I must have tried it and been hushed. On emerging from the 'tunnel' a right turn took you past the back of the houses to Gran's, the last in the block, the sequence repeated until the end of the street. The back doors led out into a yard with coal house and WC and gardens which were reached across the access path, each with a gate of its own. At the bottom of my grandparent's was a workshop and shed which I have no recollection of entering. The main feature of the garden was an exceptionally disappointing cherry tree, very large and spreading but never fruitful; someone had tried the stress inducing half-way ring barking technique but even this proved no inducement. In my teens with Gran now alone I offered to do some gardening. I made a start but only a start as the inevitable elbow bleed was the result and I never resumed. Neither of us mentioned it on future visits. It took me some years of continual trial and error before my technique improved to the extent that gardening became no more and no less haemorhagenic than any other activity.

Most years my parents had a day out at the Earl's Court motor show, I was happy to be left behind as looking at motor vehicles was not exactly my idea of an enjoyable time. Usually I'd be left with Gran and on one of these prolonged visits she provided me with a soup tureen full of water on the newspaper covered dining table for me to play with my little boats, toy cowboys and a native American in a metal canoe. I wondered if the canoe would float, of course it went straight to the bottom and this started me wondering why huge ships also made of metal could be persuaded to float, after some thought I decided to save time by looking for the answer next time I came across a suitable book. I mistrusted the opinions of those around me and even if I'd asked would not have been convinced by the answer.

Chapter 11

I learned when very young to question each statement having experienced the truth that children in particular are often lied to 'for their own good' or at least have foisted on them belief presented as fact.

The living room fireplace had a curiously bulbous black metal contraption just above the grate which I believe may have been used to regulate the amount of air getting to the burning coal and a high backed dining chair with an equally bulbous brown shiny seat. Above the seat high on the wall was a large framed photograph of Aunt Win, so they told me, as a child. She gazed at the camera holding on her lap what I much later made out to be a book. It must be that my eyesight had never been good and the truth only struck me when I was prescribed spectacles but I had always thought that the object she clutched was a large 'Christmas' tin of Quality Street chocolates though why a photograph pointing out such greed was prominently displayed puzzled me. I had seen a photograph taken at some holiday resort of Mum and Win perched on donkeys, Mum's quadruped smiling, as Mum was at that time very slight, and Win's with a strained expression, belly almost dragging on the ground at having to support a heavyweight and I chuckled as I imagined the sight when the animals took their uneven burdens off along the sand. Mum shows a face as long and woebegone as Win's donkey, perhaps she realised their juxtaposition was meant for laughter.

I upset Gran, possibly many times, but on one of the motor show visits distressingly on refusing to eat. The conflict between Mum and Gran and the deeply held conviction in most quarters that Mum was a bad cook, provoked a dilemma when Mum said 'don't be surprised if he won't eat' and Gran replied 'he will if I cook it'. If I ate Gran would be triumphant and Mum's hopeless culinary skills confirmed and if I refused to eat I would upset Gran and be an extremely ungrateful child, though that would be nothing unusual, such disapprobation being the norm when I refused food. Actually my disinclination to eat had nothing to do with anyone else as I saw it, which may well have been ungrateful, and neither was I 'seeking attention' this facile interpretation often being cited. I very rarely felt hungry, certainly not hungry enough to eat stuff I found virtually tasteless at best and at worst nauseating. If I didn't feel hungry and didn't find what was presented delicious then what was the point in struggling to force it down?

As the clock advanced to lunch time so my anxiety grew in proportion and the smell of the cooking worried me more and more. The food was brought to table and

Gran waited with a smile to watch me make a start. The comestibles I hated most were meat, apart from bacon, and cabbage yet as I'd guessed from the steamy smells from the kitchen here they were, along with potatoes, on the plate before me. This made up my mind and supported my loyal determination to back up my mother and when my parents came to collect me Gran complained bitterly about my refusal to eat, reporting my words 'I'm not eating that muck'. A terrible thing for me to say but think of the position I'd been put in by the warring parties, I should not have been required to choose sides and I loved them both.

The family had so much intolerance one toward another throughout, that my loyalty was often stretched and problematic. The aggressive tone of my refusal followed my regular pattern when pressure became intolerable and I felt threatened, jump in with a verbal, occasionally physical, attack and to hell with the possible consequences.

Most Sundays we would take Gran for a drive and picnic if the weather permitted. In my memory this ritual went on all year for a couple of years at least but it must have been curtailed during winter. We usually drove to the Cotswolds, occasionally north as far as the Trent but never into Derbyshire. Dad had acquired a large steel chest, painted it black and bought a Primus stove. The chest would be filled with the picnic paraphernalia and goodies and the picnic would be the high point of the afternoon. I can almost smell the lit mentholated spirit used to warm the burner and the roaring paraffin, warm and comforting as the water boiled for tea and Mum and Gran arranged rug, tablecloth, china and food. Good, relaxed times when Dad and I would explore a little of the fields and woodland. One lovely picnic spot I remember with affection, a little woodside clearing, adjacent a narrow winding lane, where two or three conifers had managed to establish and grow tall and straight with stumps of old branches sticking out all the way down and I was tempted to climb but Dad showed me that they were rotten and would more than likely break under my weight. After our picnic we took a walk along the lane and discovered that both sides were lined with hazel bushes and we all picked nuts to take home.

If open animosity reared its head this would be immediately after the trip as Mum muttered about Gran calling me 'her little half-back' by which she meant we shared the back seat half-and-half. Mum was convinced that this was a gentle but definite complaint that she wasn't let sit in the front alongside Dad, this could be a fact but I interpreted it as an affectionate comment and everyone had seemed happy enough as we drove along the lanes and I gazed at the spectacular views, dry stone walls, sheep and the stone built cottages; quaint and intriguing to me as their chocolate box gardens and stone fading through the years from yellow to grey invited me to speculate on the lives of those within.

A laughable indication of the rivalry between the female half of our complement was that Mum refused to wear a hat and Gran when out always did. To hear Mum revile all hats as silly was a regular occurrence. Apropos headgear, Dad also was not a fan, dismissing all caps as 'ratting hats' and using the term in a derogatory sense, as 'look at him in his ratting hat' with a tut and jerk of the chin. Not that all hats and caps were anathema. Another photo in my possession shows Dad wearing a homburg in the thirties and looking like a mate of Al Capone. He also had a soft spot for the Coventry kid's cap which apparently had a button on top and a set number of panels. Pipe smoking also led to a quiet sneer: Look at him smoking his dirty old clay (it could in fact be the finest Meerschaum) he thinks it makes him look intelligent. An individual going about his business with a fuming pipe and a flat cap roused his full contempt! Another attitude I rejected preferring to assign value not by how a person looked but their actions.

A curious aspect of our day-trips remains a tantalising puzzle. It soon became apparent that we were never going to visit anything like an organised attraction on our country drives. It's possible that Dad thought by spending money on petrol he'd done enough, but given his strangely selective shyness it's also possible that he didn't wish to interact with the staff or other visitors. Once, on noticing a pleasure boat on the Trent, full of people enjoying a trip on the river, I asked if we could take a turn, the disappointing answer was 'no' we will next time'. It was late in the day; we'd had our picnic some time before so I was content to take him at his word.

The next time we went north on our Sunday trip we went directly toward the Trent, I saw the large boat making its way down river and was excited and grateful that he'd remembered and was taking us to embark but then I noticed him watching me, when traffic allowed, in the rear view mirror as we drove further and further away from the river. Was it a Test? Did he wish me to beg? If so would I then have got my river jaunt or would he have again said no? I couldn't bring myself to ask and find out.

Though puzzled by the teasing if that was what it was he must never know how thwarted and disappointed I felt and I had to be satisfied with that. Hindsight tells me he'd probably forgotten the whole thing until he noticed the boat and hoped I'd forgotten too. If neither of us mentioned it then he could avoid whatever ordeal he anticipated.

A more pleasant afternoon saw us driving through Oxfordshire alongside a river amongst dappled shade cast by the trees that lined the bank. A little further on the lane took us higher and we found a parking space next to the wide flat stump of an oak which made a perfect picnic table. From our elevated position above the river we could watch it disappear under a water mill and race out the other side and to make the day special for me a pair of swans sped along the river from the mill gathering speed, their wings beating fast to take to the sky just below us and dwindle into the distance. We had travelled to this idyllic spot in convoy with another couple, curiously while I know that to be true who they were has gone from my memory. The grown men of the party walked down on their own to get a closer look at the mill turning to wave up to us, too far for facial recognition. Why didn't I accompany them? recovering from a knee bleed? or perhaps they had something private to discuss.

My years at Corley Open Air School had stimulated an interest in the countryside, nature in general and folk music. I used to listen every Sunday morning to a home service radio broadcast of song collected from all around Britain, As I Roved Out. Most of the performers were elderly, or at least seemed so and I very much hoped that Gran might suddenly reveal herself as a repository of ancient song and broadside but the only song I ever heard her sing a few words of was When I met Connie in the Cornfield, which turned out to be a song from the twenties jazz era, despite its title being so countrified and having the potentially stimulating feel of one of the numerous songs of seduction folk song abounds with.

Chapter 12

One word Gran used that I never heard from anyone else; she loved to see a fire when it was 'all of a gleed', an archaic dialect word meaning a glowing ember or hot coal, so while not able to supply me with folk song she gave me an old word to add to my vocabulary. A phrase she often resorted to when I insisted on sharing my, probably banal, views on this or that was 'sure to be right!' Her eyesight grew steadily worse over time due to cataracts but generally she enjoyed good health until late in life she developed appendicitis and had the vestigial sac removed. During the recovery period she was surprised to be asked the usual question a surgeon will ask to ascertain whether peristalsis has resumed. His ill-chosen words 'Have you pooped-off' mystified her as she had no idea what he was getting at until he asked a more reasonable question and she blushingly admitted she had.

Right up until the end Gran saved her small change for me and having read somewhere in my voracious but unregulated reading of a character referred to as a remittance man, in my ignorance I referred to this as my remittance. Now I understand that a remittance man is someone the family no longer wish to see but can't leave destitute, I sometimes think how crass of me to use a word I didn't fully apprehend and sometimes how instinctively intuitive, the differing interpretations of my foolishness dependent on my emotional state at the time.

Gran died in 1967 aged eighty-five. All the years I knew her she lived in Villiers Street and every time I pass down Clay Lane I think of that little terraced house I used to visit, arriving and leaving with a smile, and regret that I never visited her in hospital as she lay dying. The reason is lost in the past. Was it because of the rancour between my Uncle and Dad likely to become embarrassingly obvious even at such a time, or was I experiencing yet another internal haemorhage, maybe cowardice not wanting to see her reduced, or a further indication of my need to keep hospital and home compartmentalised? Or possibly, a combination of all or some of these things, the one certainty is that I will never know. It remains pitiful that the discord between Mum and latterly Dad and Gran should have taken the place of good family relations.

Grandad had attended Coventry College of Art in Ford Street and he could paint a sign or draw a line freehand on a van gilding his letters or paint your coat of arms on the side of your car and indeed offered to do this for Dad whether in fun or seriously I speculate. Dad would have almost certainly refused if the latter as he hated ostentation. What on earth his coat of arms would have consisted of is open to question, crossed argent spanners on a field of greasy sable?

Walter invented a crackle finish on painted surfaces but the idea was stolen and patented by a 'friend' who wrote him a note: Better luck next time Wal.

His urge to invent must have been a strong one as he once developed a cream for taming unruly hair and what better 'volunteer' to be its test pilot than his own unruly son. Dad was sent out with his hair plastered to his skull by a concoction which relied on sugar as the main ingredient. Not unexpectedly the sugary hair drew a following of wasps and flies some of which became embedded in the rapidly drying sugary cap reminiscent of the fate of ancient bees in amber. If further experiments along the same lines ensued Dad never revealed but he did tell me of the imposition suffered by means of clothing. As he grew so did the need for new clothes and he'd be taken to get a new suit. No doubt money was tight even then so economy was the order of the day and he would plead that the local cheap suit mart be avoided: No Dad, please, not Gibberd's dog hair again!

The manufacture of bicycles being the major trade in Coventry at that time Grandad found employment painting and gilding the lines that decorated the frame. He volunteered himself to collect the pads used in the applying of gold leaf by himself and his fellow workers which would be discarded onto the floor after use and the management applauded his effort to keep the floor of the workshop tidy. He would take the pads home with him each night and when a large bag had accrued have the gold extracted. Once the obvious value was realised by those who should have known from the beginning his extra earner came to an end.

He was a man of talent who loved to swim, being particularly good at the backstroke, butterfly and Australian crawl and I have a memory of seeing him, at Billing Aquadrome backstroking impressively away beer belly much in evidence.

His inventiveness could be called into action whenever needed or as the fancy took him, as when Dad was obliged to assist with the hair cream. Talented but impatient with small talk, a trait passed down to this grandson, hating to be accosted in the street or collared by what he considered silly women he gained a measure of notoriety when on a bus he was confronted by a friend of his mother. 'Oh, hello Walter I haven't seen you for ages.' To shut her up and bring potential conversation to a halt he blurted 'You're not likely to have, I've been in Australia'. Since no one in those days travelled very far the stupefied woman had nothing more to say, which was just what he intended. Later, when she asked his mother about his travels the whole story came out and he acquired the nickname Australian Wal.

Shyness could be ruled out; this was not a man to mess around with. When more silly women, this time in the form of silly tarts, by which he meant young girls, attempted to adorn him with a white feather, an accusation of cowardice imposed on men not in uniform during the first world war, he dared them to carry it through, showing them his fist with the information: See this? Put that on me and you'll get it on the end of your snout!

They went away crestfallen and I believe it's as well they did. In fact he worked for the duration in a reserved occupation at the Royal Ordinance factory on Red lane and wore a little brass badge with a representation of a field gun on it to prevent just such a confrontation.

My grandfather was very protective of his children and would never permit anyone else to physically punish them. When Dad returned from school and was noticed wincing as he touched his ear he was obliged to reveal how a teacher had boxed his ears and a large signet ring had cut him. Grandad just said 'Right, I know where he drinks; I'll have a word with him tonight.' Later, just as the man lifted his glass of whisky to his lips Grandad jabbed him in the back with a thumb held between first and second fingers sending his hand jerking, spilling the drink down his front. He was graphically advised that if he laid hands on Dad again he would find Grandad's shoe up his arse right up to the third lace-hole, a charming phrase of fair warning. Teacher apologised.

The fracas with the school attendance officer was more serious leading to fine of a florin, (twenty pence) from the magistrates but had a similar cause.

Back then when a mother gave birth at home one of the girls in the family would be kept off school to help out. Dad's sister Win was given time off for this purpose and was sent on an errand. Later there was a knock on the door and Grandad opened it to see Win crying and being hauled practically off her feet by a uniformed school attendance officer who had her by the collar and hair. 'What do you think of this naughty little girl' shaking her from side to side, 'I caught her out of school.' 'Oh yes' says Grandad, 'Take your hands off her.' When the officer complied Grandad grabbed him by his collar and the seat of his pants, ran him across the road and threw him into the river. The Sherbourne at that point had high walls on both sides so that he had to wade all the way to Swan Lane to emerge soaking wet and weary. As he went he yelled 'I'll have the law on you' and shook his fist, and reader, he kept his word. I think Grandad, certainly his son and this grandson thought it well worth a florin.

Grandad died before I left Corley and when he died in his mind he was back at work sign writing on vehicles and gesturing to hallucinatory workmates with the words 'Wheel 'em in, wheel 'em in' on his lips. Shortly before the illness which led to his death he had insisted on visiting me at Corley on what was apparently a blazing hot day and on the return journey he didn't feel well. He had said 'I must go and see Derek.' perhaps he felt close to the end. I clearly remember mother breaking the news with tears in her eyes but more tellingly none in mine.

Chapter 13

For many years this bothered me, Grandad was important to me but I was unable to cry either then or later in private and this puzzled me at the time and worried me later. On reading of a dastardly character in a novel I wondered if I too might be an 'unfeeling brute'. I came to realise retrospectively that I had, when very young, been obliged to suppress my emotions when Mum came to visit me in hospital as she impressed on me 'They'll stop me coming to see you if you cry', a powerful injunction and, after all, I had been deracinated and the things and people of home, although only a few miles away might have been a thousand, 'now' and 'here' being enough for a small boy to cope with. The finality of a funeral might have encouraged me to grieve but this was not suggested, or so I assume; it is possible that those in authority may have refused permission as they did with my brother's wedding.

My parent's first child, Sydney Leslie was born October 1930, fourteen years my senior and for the first years of my life my hero. It didn't take too long for me to learn the truth that he was *not* capable of doing anything in the world if he chose to but I never lost my love for him and was devastated when he died, aged not quite fifty, in January 1980 a victim of malignant melanoma and the cerebral secondary it spawned.

It was not lost on me that my mother had outlived three of her four children, a cruel reversal of the norm and that I, the one prescribed an early death from the consequences of chronic illness, should have been the one to survive. But hey, what's random is random, or is as far as we know....

I know a little of his exploits as a boy, told to me by himself or my parents. He owned an air pistol and once shot a mouse with it, a feat generating as much pride as if it had been a marauding beast about to devour him, he never mentioned how close the poor creature had allowed him to creep!

Another small individual of the rodent persuasion was captured by Syd and his cronies and put on trial for undermining the war effort by stealing grain, a heinous crime during a time of strict rationing. The verdict was inevitable, the jury partisan and the defence probably non-existent, the micentious verdict of death by hanging was implemented forthwith. This act I did not approve of. Another poor mouse was inadvertently gassed when Syd's wellington boots which had been out in the cold were brought in and warmed by the fire. The creature was found newly dead when he put on the boots, it must have hidden in there and been overcome by the heat and rubber fumes.

Once when snow lay on the ground the local boys including Syd, rounded up a bunch of canines and tried to form a dog team to pull a sledge, he never went into the results but my imagination supplied the details with fighting dogs pulling in all directions leading to utter failure.

Motor vehicles played a large part in both Syd's and my life and two stories about pleasure trips in a car when Syd was younger were often repeated.

Either I have forgotten the preamble or was never told so don't know why the family including Gran and Grandad drove so far but at some point enough beer had been consumed to require a stop for Grandad to relieve his bladder. After what must have seemed an age to my brother as a boy Grandad emerged from the bushes and on getting into the car said to him 'You've had a long ride' to elicit the obviously incredulous response 'You've had a long pee'! On a trip out with the Sprouls in yet another car, a convertible, Syd and Cousin Rose were left in the car with crisps and pop whilst the adults went into a pub for a brief respite from the road. When they emerged and drove off it became apparent that the two inquisitive cousins had been experimenting with various levers and buttons in flagrant disobedience and the roof of the convertible lifted up into the air like a sail. This was told to me with a smile but I don't suppose it was so funny at the time!

Dad often told the cautionary tale concerning local kids, possibly including Syd, who broke into an ammunition store associated with the barrage balloon or anti aircraft site behind the houses and across a field or two and stole a grenade, stored without fuse. Someone had the bright idea of lighting a fire and placing the grenade on it to set it off and going closer when nothing happened was injured as it exploded. Dad and others raced out and the boy was carried home, alive but blinded. Over a number of years, digging on The Dump for various reasons, I unearthed three, at different times, live 303 rifle rounds and assume these came from the ammo store raid.

The war time bombing was escaped by resorting to air-raid shelters either communal or my uncle's and when fuel was available driving out into the countryside. On a dark night this could be quite perilous though safer than remaining in the city as the car's headlights operated through a slit and did very little to light the way. Though dimmed by the expedient nevertheless they had to be switched off altogether when a 'lost' German bomber appeared to be following the lights.

Mum, Dad, Gran and Grandad were in the car and they drove on for a short time then stopped. They heard the distinctive sound of the bomber's synchronised engines begin to fade and were then shocked when a stick of bombs exploded a couple of fields away, the crew obviously thinking the car had reached home.

The family home suffered bomb damage when a chunk of masonry composed of a mass of bricks and mortar crashed through the roof and lodged halfway through the ceiling of the bedroom where my parents slept when not sheltering. The degree of exhaustion, in common with so many others, that my parents experienced explains how they spent several nights sleeping with the masonry wedged in the ceiling directly above their heads until Dad on wakening looked up. 'We're silly buggers that could work loose any time!'

Making do and mending, queuing and bartering, missing sleep and worrying and on one occasion biting and scarring Dad this was my mother's war. All this and running a non-labour-saving home as women did back then.

The biting and scarring was accomplished on the night a bomber crashed in flames out toward Ansty. The plane came over flying low and I believe on fire and passed directly over the house, sounding in trouble, the light was switched off and everyone ran to the back door to see it. Mum wrenched open the door, looked up saw the plane and excitedly turned her head shouting 'here it is' and neatly removed a piece of flesh from Dad's nose. 'Well it was his own fault, it was dark in the blackout and he shouldn't have been standing on my heels.' Dad bore the scar of the inadvertent cannibalism for the rest of his days. Not that he bore a grudge or worried that she might have got the taste for on the 27th. November 1944 I was born and before the next year was out the ordeal was over and peace returned.

Dad took some months off work and lived on money he'd saved during wartime, as he remarked to me when recalling this, he'd worked extremely hard during the course of the war and was due a rest. A cause for complaint was the delayed repayment of the extra tax extracted by the wartime government, Post War Credits. Promised repayment 'after the war' Dad, like so many others, had no idea just how vague the promise was, the credits not finally repaid until 1972. He had joined the home guard but refused to carry on when the officer in charge had the men hiding in gateways on Ansty Road while he dodged about with a pearl handled revolver. 'That silly bugger will get us all killed' his verdict on the man's competence.

He was directed into the repair of aircraft engines as a foreman for the duration. As a first class mechanic his occupation was reserved. The corrupt practices prevalent in the motor trade, which he so much abhorred, were maintained into the war and the aircraft engine repair shop was no exception. A great many workers in the factories he'd been associated with had gained employment through the old pals system. 'It's not what you know but who you know.' And many of those he termed muckanic were taken on via the buying one of the 'gaffers' a drink method. This was confirmed for me when some years after my boyhood I overheard, in a pub, this: Ah, he's a good lad, ah kid's gonna get 'im in at the 'umber, 'e drinks wi' one o' the gaffers. Dad would often tell me of his disgust when one of the muckanics came to him and asked for another bolt and on being asked why he needed it admitted to losing one by dropping it into the engine and not being able to find it! The potentially disastrous outcome had the repaired engine had been fitted to an aircraft can be readily imagined.

Chapter 14

Dad wanted the employee dismissed but was told by his own supposedly superior that this would not be happening because the worker was the protégée of someone even higher up the scale. Disgusted on being told this he wished to resign but this was, as he well knew, forbidden during the war.

A friend of his came to him some time after this incident and took him into a store room, up a ladder and showed him a space, constructed by moving boxes, furnished with blankets and pillows so that although being paid extra for working nights it was possible to disappear for a nap now and then, several employees taking turns. He was invited to join the scheme but declined, keeping quiet about it presumably for friendship and chagrin at the dangerously debonair mechanic being kept on the payroll.

It was indicative of his commitment that Dad had agreed to work nights as he had refused on many occasions before the war. He lost jobs because of his attitude but could not be dissuaded from his insistence on day work only. At one company he was advised that nights were compulsory, it was his turn and it meant an extra thruppence an hour, he asked for his cards and left to start another job the next day.

Many years later when retired and living in Cornwall his neighbour took him to a vintage car rally and he became very interested in one of the cars and asked the owner to lift the bonnet and there, as he hoped, on the immaculately clean engine was a brass plaque reading: This engine built by S. Haughton. The owner of the car was astonished at the coincidence and overjoyed to meet the man who put the engine together and I had no difficulty in imagining Dad's pleasure and quiet satisfaction. The make and model I don't recall but suppose the vehicle came from the time of his first job after leaving school.

Starting work at thirteen, he had to stand on a box to reach the work bench, short in stature perhaps, but as he told me wiry and strong, a quick learner he soon became a skilled mechanic building motor engines while standing on that box. These were the days before Henry Ford's track system so that one man, or boy, built each complete engine. No apprenticeship was served and he was often contemptuous of many who had having himself been thrown in at the deep end and expected to get on with it, he knew that very often it was necessary to improvise a method when the usual idea failed to produce the desired result. To Dad a good man was one who knew his job, whatever that job might be and he distrusted anyone with mere paper qualifications as he saw it, and no time at all for anyone who had risen through influence rather than ability.

His chief leisure activity, apart from newspaper reading and the pub, was alternate Saturdays throughout the season standing on Spion Kop at Highfield Road to watch Coventry City, a waste of time I thought when young. I recall telling him, at the age of ten, I had no interest in football and he replied 'You will when you're older'. Many of his predictions remain unfulfilled but how right he was about that. Play up Sky Blues! He also advised against following the club to Walsall's ground for an away match, 'they piddle up your back', he'd seen it happen.... He had a favourite football joke and any club could be the unfortunate butt: They had two china-men play for them at one time, Wi Woon Wuns and How L'ong Sins. Not particularly hilarious but typical of the man, a frustrated performer; who, at home, would enter the room, strike an attitude and launch into snippets of dialogue or a song.

'What's the time? Just struck a copper bald headed'. 'It's been forty years since I had a bit of pork, but I can run as well as walk!' This last would finish with a stage chuckle of evil intent and might be followed by 'Feed him on tomatoes, he'll never have a cough, let him smell the good fresh air' or the chorus of the Harry Champion song Boiled Beef & Carrots, which might be followed by 'a quarter pound of ham please and cut it thin it's for the lodger'.

Often he would give us a brief monologue with voices off achieved by raucous murmurings into cupped hands: T'is Minnie the Moocher's wedding day, ten thousand pounds I'll give away. (voices off) Hooray, Hooray for the old squire. On second thoughts (with a twirl of an imaginary moustache) I think it best to stick it back in the old oak chest. (voices off) Why you lousy old, miserly bustard you.

His sudden bursts of facetiousness delighted me, mostly caused by his own pleasure in what he sang or recited:

Go to bed Tom
Go to Bed Tom
Go to Bed, go to bed
Go to bed Tom

He would accompany this with a beaten rhythm on any available piece of furniture, followed by a smile of satisfaction. This was, of course his version of a nursery rhyme but this was never pointed out to me and I only learned the truth of this many years into adulthood, on reading a collection of more or less obscure nursery rhymes.

Jokes he very rarely told, and those he did were often repeated. An elderly, very dignified lady stands up as the train is about to pull into the station. The train stops with a jerk, throwing her onto her behind, as she gets to her feet the conductor announces the station. 'Ascot, Ascot, and with a blush she replies 'No young man only bruised'.

A man, on a station platform has an urgent call of nature and on reaching the Gents finds it locked with a notice advising it as under repair, not being able to contain the overwhelming urge a moment longer he squats down behind a luggage trolley and let's fly. On standing he sees for the first time that he's been observed by three porters. 'Tut-tut' says the senior bod, 'the station master won't have this.' 'Won't he? Well, why don't you lot share it out amongst yer!'

The fact that these jokes are concerned with behinds or that which may be extruded therefrom may indicate why I never heard the rest of his cache of humour.

Often he would break into a vaguely disturbing song. Was this a reference back to an incident in his childhood, the words sticking because so relevant to his memory of a specific event?

Is the protagonist politically or criminally motivated? Whichever or whatever I was always on his side.

Down our street there's been a blooming riot
And the police they cannot keep 'em quiet
They're a waitin' there for me!
They're a waitin' there for me!
They'll have to wait 'til the moon turns green
And whiskers grow on margarine
Ha ha, he he, I'm not going back you see
For, if anybody knows a thing or two
It's me, me, me, me, me!

I have no skill to render the tune and can't vouch for the lineation but I remember it clearly word for word.

Amusing stories were often repeated a favourite of both of us concerned a holiday at Blackpool back in his early manhood with his mate George. They shared a room in a boarding house, a typical boarding house run by a typical seaside landlady of the time who pestered and jumped on the pair for every minor infraction of the myriad house rules.

On the last day of the holiday George bought a pair of kippers and on vacating the room the two young men took great delight in pinning them to the under surface of a table. The results had to be imagined as the elusive smell of rotting fish became pervasive and the complaints to the landlady grew. Personally I would have used the back of the wardrobe as the kippers' resting place, more difficult to find. Oh, the flies, the possible flies!

We know what all work does so I can only applaud the playful shenanigans he regaled me with, in stories of the lighter side of factory life.

I'll begin with the well known Long Stand Hammer. This mythical tool would often be required to be fetched when a youngster first started in the shop. 'We'll need the long stand hammer for this job, go and ask Smithy for it, over there, see?' Our callow friend asks Smithy and is told to wait, after a time Smithy recalls that Tommy has it, Tommy says wait and some minutes later suddenly remembers that Brownie borrowed it and the waiting continues, the process repeated until the newcomer realises how long he has had to stand waiting. If still unwary a trip to the furnace for a bucket of sparks may enlighten him.

One such apprentice on being sent for sparks was not to be taken in and finding an old bucket placed hot coals inside and came back dropping handfuls of iron filings onto the coals producing sparks and the realisation that this 'kid' wasn't so easily fooled. Two further incidents ensured he didn't last long in the job.

To the astonishment of the others a car was seen to be driving around the test track by itself and a crowd gathered to marvel. This vehicle had a slit through which it was possible to peer at the road ahead when crouched down out of view, thus the car seemed to be driven by a phantom, when the truth became apparent he was severely ticked off. This did not prove much of a warning and his next exploit earned him his dismissal.

Chapter 15

He tied up another apprentice and hooked and hoisted him up to run him along on the apparatus for lifting engines, amusing for him but a foolish and dangerous stunt which won him the immediate presentation of the sack.

Another older but no less gullible newcomer to the workshop on receiving his first pay packet with its list of deductions asked a workmate what HAM, for which he'd been deducted a small sum, meant. 'Blimey, you lucky sod, hey! Come and look at this, only here a week and he's won the ham'. The others played along and the victim was assured that he would get his ham at the end of the next week.

A large ham of shaped wood was made in the wood shop and painted to resemble the joint, wrapped up in newspaper and foisted on the poor dupe with many further comments about his good fortune. Other eatables cod, capon, and imps, have a role in the last three that Dad entertained me with.

A foreman with bulging eyes much disliked by the men had, as part of his duties to check the level of oil in a large drum or vat and would every day lift the lid and peer inside. By trial and error allied to engineering skills and maths cod heads purchased expressly for the purpose were affixed, with wire and cork so that they floated in the oil as though the fish were sticking their heads out of the depths. Along came the foreman, from that day on known as Cod's-Eyes, lifted the lid, dropped it with a snort of disbelief and staggered back, pale and shaking.

The capons were, I believe, a form of Christmas bonus and the men chose the one they thought best. A couple of weights were inserted into one of the birds and sure enough the greediest most grasping individual dived at the row of fowl and lifting them in turn nabbed the heaviest for himself, making no comment after the return to work.

The imps referred to are those tiny liquorice pieces sold in small tins as an aid to lubricating the throat. One of the workmates kept an open tin on his bench and another would take a pinch of a few without the courtesy of asking. Becoming tired of this the inadvertent purveyor decided he would teach a lesson and get his revenge. A walk in the countryside provided him with sheep droppings which chopped into little pieces with a razorblade looked sufficiently like the tiny lozenges as to fool the casual snaffler. Sure enough the open tin of 'sheep shits' was rifled with a grin, when the culprit remarked 'Umm, not as nice as the last lot!'.

Later, when Dad and his partners were involved in Coventry Sheet Metal he would have nothing to do with the corrupt practices endemic in the city, where small concerns like his competed for contracts from motor manufacturers, other businesses and local government. The only incentive as far as I know, that he agreed to were the Christmas drink gifts of whisky or port for those 'gaffers' who had favoured the firm over the year and those most likely to in the future, even this he was not entirely happy with. He maintained that the firm's reputation for promptness, skilfully carried out work and general integrity should be enough to attract work, an opinion that caused friction between him and his partners who favoured a more relaxed approach including wining and dining some slimy individual, a horrible prospect, when grubbing for contracts. I vividly recall his anger as he told me that someone had turned up at the premises expecting to have his ailing car fixed for nothing in return for 'promises'. This individual had demanded services that the company did not provide, having been told to do so by the company secretary, remarking that Dad had better do as the boss had ordered. 'I've told him, on many occasions, that we don't work on vehicles, either mechanical or bodywork and yet he still sends them', the 'he' being his company secretary and brother. On at least one occasion he returned from Red lane incandescent to rail against my uncle's incompetence as the telephone bill had not been paid.

Dad was proud of the fact that he had taken time to learn metal work on starting the firm, 'I changed my trade, taking the first few months to do it, and we don't repair cars.' He made various 'apprentice pieces' during that time, tankards and model companion sets and obviously learned a great deal, so I for one understood his reluctance to go back to something others might have thought his only talent. To my sorrow someone removed the items my parents had of his making before my mother, who outlived him, died so I have no physical memorabilia just 'visual' memories of the brass and copper work, and a key he made for an old chiming clock he'd got hold of somehow. The winding key was missing so he'd made a new one, the clock is long gone but I still have the key. Two 'keyholes' adorned the clock-face one for the movement and the other for the chimes. He very quickly found the chimes an annoyance and let the mechanism run down, then found that occasionally he'd applied the key to the wrong keyhole and the chimes would be off again, this he rectified by removing the chime bars so that where before the clock would whirr in preparation for the chimes it would make the same fuss much to my amusement then emit only a series of clicks as the hammers fell. I would await this if we had guests anticipating the puzzled looks on their faces.

The many differences of opinion between him and my uncle over the running of the firm were just the tip of an iceberg, down to sibling rivalry, the usual elder brother younger brother in fighting with my uncle favoured as the youngest child of a family often is. This was one cousin's interpretation of the family dynamic, having seen at first hand how Gran and her two sons interacted when they all had a meal together. 'Your Gran never offered any praise to your Dad it was all Bob, and Syd noticed'. Dad, me and my uncle all went to the Sky Blues home matches.... a family occasion?

No, sadly we arrived and left separately, I had a season ticket in the stand, my uncle stood on the terracing below me and we would exchange waves before the match while Dad stood on Spion Kop. This was when I was a few years older and is examined more deeply in the book about my adult exploits, The Rest of My Bleeding Life.

Football by which I mean Association Football, soccer, not Rugby which was anathema to my father and which he referred to as arse and whistle, played a major role in his life until he left the city of his birth to move to Cornwall. Coventry City F C started life as the works team Singer FC in the late eighteen eighties and changed its name to Coventry City in 1898. Dad supported the team from a young age his extended family involved once a year. Matches were often played on Christmas day morning at that time and the last league match played on the 25th December was at Bloomfield Road, Blackpool versus Blackburn in 1965.

If there was a home match on Christmas day the family, who had gathered for the festivities, would leave the lunch to slowly cook and, women and children too, go 'up the city' as a group. The significance of the womenfolk attending with the men and boys was always emphasised as this was the only time it happened in the season and was talked of with amused tolerance, much being made of the offside rule as an impediment to female enjoyment and understanding of the game, it being impossible to explain the seeming complexity to women.

The facts were of course, somewhat different; if the menfolk failed to explain the rules of the game it reflected their own poor skill at communication. Women's football was growing in popularity and had drawn a crowd, on Boxing Day 1920, of fifty-three thousand, not in Coventry I hasten to add, and had provoked a negative response from the Football Association who banned women's teams from playing on Football League grounds right up until 1971, ostensibly because 'The game of football is quite unsuitable for females and ought not to be encouraged'. The truth is that the dinosaurs in charge panicked and stampeded over the cliff of their own ineptitude – unfair? A little perhaps – the world had been changed forever by the 1914-18 war, so many men were mobilised and died that women had been required to assert themselves, no wonder the establishment felt the need to claw its way back to the top, needing to reassert due deference not on competence but on gender.

Having joined the football league at the start of the 1919/20 season the team were without a win after nineteen matches and the home match on Christmas day marked the first ever league win for the Bantams. Whether the family attended I don't know for sure but I believe it may have been so.

Chapter 16

The bi-annual family excursion round the corner (or two) to Highfield road continued up until the Second World War when the family tradition ceased, the Football League being suspended for the duration. The Christmas family get together ceased too, survival taking precedence, such a pity as I would have enjoyed the chaos, clashing personalities in abeyance and stories of past days and people with all the males sleeping on the floor of the front room in a made up 'round bed' and the women upstairs sleeping 'top-to-toe'. When I asked that the joint celebration be resumed as I'd not been around to experience it Dad would tell me: No the war stopped all that!

I can't know what else the war put a stop to although I suspect many friendships and alliances among the family may have been involved. I know that certain relatives who had once played a part, major or minor, in my parent's life were only ever mentioned in passing. I only ever met, and that briefly, one or two of dad's friends, Arthur L, who had started, and failed at, various business ventures including his own football pool company and Ivor R father of another haemophiliac I often spent time with in hospital. Mum often laughed at Arthur and I once attempted to do the same, Dad sternly and with obvious displeasure flashed 'At least he's a trier'! Dad would presumably have denied friendship as on several occasions he told me I had no friends, only acquaintances. As I grew older I would have to bite my tongue to prevent the obvious rejoinder, you speak for yourself.

One' acquaintance' of Dad's, Stan B, owned a couple of pet shops in Birmingham and a red setter which on a visit we took for a run in Sutton Park, galloping back to us it knocked me over and of course I was asked if I was alright. I told them yes, as I always did, but I wouldn't know if a bleed had started until later. In fact I was alright, no bleed. The Browns who had moved to Totnes, Devon and the Nashes who may or may not have been distant family, I was always encouraged to call them Aunt and Uncle, were obviously on friendly terms with Dad but none of these people lived in Coventry, at least in my youth.

Drinking companions did not count as friends anyway, and when he gave up pub going they disappeared and it's possible that this was the origin of his assertion that one only had acquaintances not friends. One of these 'turned out to be a bit of a rat' according to him, I found out much later that he had been revealed as homosexual, one of the many ways of becoming rat like in Dad's eyes. Another drinking crony got into the habit of borrowing one pound on a Tuesday and paying it back out of his pay on Friday and this carried on until his last knock at the door one Friday evening.

Dad knew who it was and what was coming so, typically, sent Mum to answer the door and pass on the message that the pound had travelled between them so frequently that he didn't know which of them it belonged to and to keep the pound then you won't have to ask again.

The nightly pub going ceased abruptly and never resumed on Dad feeling ill and dizzy, almost falling from scaffolding where the firm was installing ducting they'd fabricated in a local car factory. This worrying episode he blamed on alcohol consumption and so no more Devonshire Arms. That was his explanation for the end of the nightly ritual of a meal, a read of the evening paper, a wash and a suit and off to the pub until chucking out time. There may of course have been more to it.

Far from being staid and stern at home, especially in music hall mode, he nevertheless had standards that he demanded of himself and others and behaviour frowned on was not tolerated. On emerging from the Devon with family members including Grandad decisive action chastised a younger man who bumped into Grandad and snarled at him to: Get out of the way, you old bastard. Oh ah? says my father grabs him by the shoulder turns him round and with one blow knocks him down and out. This was told to me not by Dad but another relative who had been in the group. The swift response was unusual as Dad would more often allow upsetting trifles to fester until he had a disproportionate outburst, only then would you know that he disapproved of your behaviour or attitude and had over some considerable time. This accounts for what I felt as an unpredictable nature; although one cousin insists he was a straightforward man, the inference being that I never understood him because I wasn't straightforward myself! No one is without contradictions in life or character and so I take the implied criticism. Dad would have done the same only to explode at a later date.

The man was no cardboard cut-out but considerably less than straightforward; I never saw him enter a shop or purchase anything although he must have done as he would occasionally produce a bag of wine gums or Murray mints and offer me one making sure to hold the bag so that only one could be taken the others concealed in his fist, a preventative to me taking two or another example of warding off the fever which might have been caught from my grubby fingers? At the first site of Coventry Sheet Metal, French's Yard, Godiva Street he got to know a woman who kept a shop, Mrs. Cook known by him as Cookie, 'Here' he'd say to me 'Cookie sent you this.' this being a bar of chocolate or some such sweet. The annual ten shilling box of fireworks and the surprise of an Easter egg one year may have been purchased from the same source, the fireworks always superb, the egg old stock with an unappetising white exudate reminiscent of mildew which entered the house and then the bin on the same day. I never knew him to visit a doctor preferring a trusted pharmacist for ointment, Golden Eye, to treat 'arc eye' from work and the black soap acquired to treat a skin condition. This soap provided a lesson in chemistry as it ate into the aluminium dish it was left in for some weeks and when I eventually removed it to the rubbish bin thin towers of white powder grew up in the dish, I worked it out that the soap contained sulphur which reacted with the aluminium to produce aluminium sulphate or that was my guess.

I recall how he kept me on tenterhooks when the annual school trip came round. Those going on the trip would have to get to the railway station around eight in the morning and I would ask Dad if he would drive me there when the day came round, he always said he didn't know, he might but he didn't know. As the morning drew closer he still didn't know and he didn't know right up to the day before. He always went out early to Red Lane to open up the gates so it shouldn't have been any trouble, did he know how much of a problem it gave me? Perhaps it was another example of his often repeated instruction not to make his arrangements for him.

For a man involved in running a business he seemed remarkably retiring when it came to confronting or merely carrying out everyday negotiations with others. His car unavailable, he would walk rather than use public transport as the bus conductor, paid to collect fairs, might talk to him and he didn't want to hear silly comments about the weather. The car was always parked around the back in the garage ostensibly because those who parked outside the front of their house were showing off. Ostentation and swank to him were ever anathema though I suspect that once again he feared being spoken to. If in a hurry he'd leave the car out front for a few minutes though his reluctance would be in no doubt as he vigorously complained to Mum.

He'd rush up the path, ineffectively try the front door which he knew was never left unlocked and crack away at the knocker. On being let in his distress would show in a ridiculous accusation about being kept waiting as other people could see him having to knock on his own front door and when Mum, not unnaturally, advised him to get a key cut his eyes would bulge and with his trade – mark quiver of the head tell her he didn't want to be seen using a key on his own front door. Perhaps a footman well placed to open and usher in as he came up the path was required but no, much too ostentatious. Once again Mum would announce that he was a funny man and that his mother was to blame.

Answering a knock was also a huge problem to the man. in position waiting for Mum to get home with his cigarettes, he wouldn't dream of solving the dilemma by popping to the local shops, if he saw someone approaching the gate he would run across the front room to the dividing door and then try to stroll to the back-door and go out before the knock came. This was highly amusing to me and if the knockee was quick he wouldn't quite make it. When younger I would already be on my feet anticipating the knock and having to answer it but when older I would tease him by staying in my seat and making him tell me there was someone at the door when I'd say as he was on his feet perhaps he'd better go and see who was there.

Chapter 17

Answer it; answer it he'd reply head quivering, eyes bulging before exiting and quietly shutting the door behind him.

His reluctance to do anything that might conceivably lead to ridicule or confrontation may be further deduced from an incident that those told of it find hard to believe.

Before Coventry Sheet Metal he bought, repaired and refurbished vehicles before selling them on, at home at the bottom of the garden. Re-sprays of panels meant a multi-coloured corrugated iron wall to one side of the garage and a stout beam inside for the lifting of engines. An engine being beyond repair and a new one needed left Dad with a problem. How to buy the thing and get it home? The answer was to have it stowed in the old pram by the vendor and to push it all the way home, this presenting him with many difficulties, not least piloting a heavy and unwieldy pram in the road, he sent Mum to carry out the onerous task and this achieved he had nothing to complain of, the engine arriving in one piece. No interaction with the vendor to disturb his equilibrium concern for the welfare of the engine his only thought. Whether Mum carried out the imposition willingly or not was hard to tell from her description which had an element of pride but also reiterated yet again her assertion that he was a funny man and that it was Gran's fault. If I repeat this over again it merely reflects the many times she gave her verdict.

I never heard the whole story so don't know how or why but Dad got so drunk one night that he couldn't drive and fell asleep in the car. Whatever the circumstances Mum drove them both home all the way from Hinckley without incident never having been taught to drive and certainly illegally, all the way in first gear, not knowing how to operate the clutch. His comment whenever she mentioned it: She ruined the engine! 'Ah yes, but I got us home *and* without an accident'. This last a reference to his not being so lucky on a trip back from Hinckley on his own, not soused but lightly marinated. He drove round a sharp bend and straight into a lorry that had been parked without lights on a dark night. His vehicle had a small metal box with a sticking out switch for turning the windscreen wipers on and off at just above head height as most cars did back then. Thrown forward and up by the impact his head came into contact with box and switch causing a long gash just above the eyebrow, fortunately missing the eye. This left a prominent scar under which rose a large bulging cyst, never mentioned but worried over as a possible tumour. Add to this the scarred nose from

Mum taking a bite in the blackout and a hole or pit in the jawline caused, I was persuaded, not by a bullet hole but an abscessed tooth and he certainly bore the signs of a life not without incident. What I never saw was the 'curly' hair Mum fell for in their younger days, perhaps she meant wavy but anyway it was always flattened and tamed by the application of water and cut at home to avoid talking to a barber.

His triple scarred physog and Mum's chewed up arm led me to an imaginative story indulged in just before sleep of nights when young. My parents were not who they purported to be but Eva Braun and Adolf Hitler blown up and scarred when sneaking out of their bunkered existence and accommodated here in a new life in gratitude for Hitler's help in defeating himself with incompetence. Just one of the flights of fancy I beguiled sleep with!

He must have made a friend of my uncle by marriage, or perhaps even he only attained acquaintance level, as they were known within the family as Minner (minnow) and Maggot for their fishing exploits, bringing home at one point two carp wrapped in wet newspaper. Finding the fish to be alive they placed them in the large rainwater tank on top of the kitchen extension part of the Church Lane house they occupied, a sensible use of a resource. The fish lived happily there for some time and local kids would ask to see them which could only be achieved by standing on the WC seat and opening the window in the bathroom.

Dad would often repeat the story of how, on a fishing expedition to a river in Northamptonshire, they had to climb over a fence onto obviously private property. 'I don't think we should be doing this, look at that sign, keep out!' unperturbed came the reply 'Ahh, it's alright, I know the owner.' They hadn't been fishing long until a grim faced imposing figure strode toward them and before the tweedy individual could launch into an unpleasant diatribe uncle jumped in with 'Good afternoon, old pal!' This friendly greeting was ignored and met with the hard hearted response 'Don't old pal me you bugger! Pack up your rods and get out'. The story was told with a smile but at the time knowing my father he would have been mortified at being a trespasser who had ignored a warning but also for choosing to believe my uncle.

Jim was a motor town Ananias – I refer to the city of my birth as motor town – a disgraceful liar, often drunk. He was also one of my favourite uncles and although I didn't see him often his exploits, as reported to the family, filled me with delight providing a welcome antidote to the stifling assumed probity reddening the features of other elders and betters as when Dad brought home a large volume which comprised information on every address in the city including the persons living there. This was not census results, though what exactly it was or how it came into his hands I never found out. It was intimated that his possession of it was only temporary and to be kept quiet about. Both parents pored over this book with obvious delight, 'Ah, I knew it, I always said they weren't married!' or 'There you are look, I told you he wasn't the father.' This joyous pouncing on other people's secrets and lies sickened me.

Mum would shake her head over my uncle's lies but to give my father his due, however wild the untruth he would defend his brother-in-law: You have to realise, Jim's a romancer, and it's just his way. Take no notice!

Tales of attempted seduction by much younger women, bogus claims of acquaintance, deeds exotic and erotic were his conversational stock, not meant as vicious but part entertainment, part wishful thinking and part self-generated ego boosting, a great deal of the time generated by tongue loosening booze. His most hilarious romance, at least I found it hilarious, was informing the other local reprobates and anyone else foolish enough to listen and take it seriously, that my father, his partners and work force were in fact employed by him, money man and sleeping partner and the return on his investment not being quite what he hoped for he was tempted to withdraw and allow the firm to fold.

Preposterous, outrageous, the verbal response from others, huge glee from me and a brief tut-tut, an upward jerk of the head and his usual defence of the man followed by the rehearsal of stories of various unfortunate exploits from Dad. Nights Jim spent in police cells after drunk and disorderly arrest with magistrate court appearances. The cells having windows, always half open but too small to allow escape at pavement level, Dad would go from one to the other calling my uncle and when he got a response drop cigarettes down to him.

The story I loved to hear concerned a drunken night when, after being refused entry to his home or finding it outside his power to locate it, he caused a panic by going to my Gran's house and sleeping, seated on the pan of the outside WC. The house was without indoor plumbing and being an early riser, Gran came out and on opening the door screamed, seeing a shadowy figure lurking in the early dawn. Lights no doubt went on and heads appeared through hastily thrown up windows as the local scandal-mongers or concerned resident's gossip seeking radar lit up at the prospect of mayhem or at least It's potential. The poor man screamed too, startled from a beer induced sleep and who knows what dream or nightmare buzzing around his no doubt, by now, pounding skull. Who, what where?

The real shock, horror came not via Jim but his son, when Dad arriving home announced on entering: I've got to find Jim! 'Ohh-er, whatever for!' says mum. 'It's Mark; he's been defying the Gran!' The grim look with which this was said and the tightly clamped lips which followed along with Mum's indrawn breath, wide eyes and her left hand up to her face, as was the wont of women given mildly shocking news, I found amusing but knew when to suppress a snigger. He would not be drawn on what the terrible act of defiance by his nephew consisted of, at least not in my presence, but I imagined a circus act, Gran with chair and whip and Mark as the lion refusing to back away or jump up onto a platform.

Of course Dad having to take the trouble to find Jim really meant Mum and straightaway she said 'I'll go and find him'.

Chapter 18

The outcome of Mark's mysterious and horrible behaviour and its aftermath I don't recall and was probably never privy to but yes, find Jim she did.

Mark three years older than me could be a pest and once tied me to a lamppost and left me there also mutilating my teddy bear. Later when he lived with us for a time he kept me from entering the house by lobbing marbles at me from the upstairs windows. On the other hand he once rode his bike to Gulson Road Hospital, ran up the rickety fire escape and passed to me a pile of comics through a window.

He lived with Gran after his mother, Aunt Win, died of quinsy in March of 1945, of course I don't remember her as I was only four months old at the time but I know my father must have missed her, as did Uncle Bob who adored her, although she was never mentioned in the house presumably my mother still harboured negative feelings. Placed in a cupboard was a homemade green leather bag unfinished attributed to aunt Win, something she was working on when she died, or that's what Mum told me, I never mentioned it to Dad and he never mentioned it or his sister.

Occasionally the subject of Jim's lip would be given an airing, not lip in the sense of impudence or inappropriate chatter but his physical lip which had suffered some kind of mysterious trauma.

The full story I was not privy to as I only caught the end of the conversation on entering the room. 'I don't feel sorry for him, it's his own fault' snaps Mum and Dad, noticing my entrance turns away his head and says nothing. Not wanting to provoke a negative response I contain my curiosity and speculate: A smack in the chops, a disease with lifestyle origins?

The other recurring conversation piece, if a relationship may be viewed as an object, was also said to be deserved. 'Ah, he'll have to go on paying until the lad's grown up.' What for, you reasonably ask? Here's the story as overheard by me: Jim 'took up with' a woman, whether they married or not is beside the point, but from my research I believe it was so, anyway, a child was involved, a boy. On returning home late one night to the home they shared, he found the locks had been changed and unable to gain entrance he'd given up and removed himself.

'Fancy letting her get away with that! He was within his rights to break in.' True or not the story was that he just accepted the situation. Subsequently he was forced to admit abandonment and pay maintenance to the woman and as inferred by Dad also for the boy possibly not his own.

It may seem that tattered remnants of the misfortunes and mistakes of others were forever being examined, repaired, ironed flat and hung on the wall as warnings and moral pointers, if so the analysis is not entirely undeserved. I proved impervious and have gone my own way endeavouring to let nothing 'mar the merriment' as I 'fair on my long fool's errand to the grave.' These pages are not about me however but the stories told to me and the memories I retain of others.

Oxford's Churchill Hospital afforded me the opportunity to meet many other haemophiliacs and although I've not retained many of their names I do remember several and the some of their stories. At that time one of the mid-strength analgesics was Ponstan, quite popular among the ward's haemophiliacs although new to me. James, another haemophiliac as all were in the four-bedder when asked what he wanted for pain absentmindedly replied, two Durex. I see, came the reply, and what do you want for pain.....

James had been stuck in hospital since childhood, when his parents, as he told me, abandoned him to the system, losing touch as he was shunted from one hospital to another. Continual bed rest led his joints to seize up and that might have been his fate for the rest of his life but for an enlightened intervention occasioning his rescue and transfer to the Churchill where he was receiving proper care and physiotherapy. He told me he had only once received physiotherapy when in a previous hospital when he'd got to know an exceptionally friendly nurse. Sex, he told me, is the best physio you can get!

A couple of years later, now fully mobile, out in the community, with a job in accountancy it seemed he'd triumphed over the neglectful stupidity and abandonment endured in his past and I celebrated his victory. This was not the end however.

I learned that his landlady had refused to accept him back to his rented room after an admission for a bleed leaving him homeless. My anger when told was taken out unfortunately on the hospital chaplain who had found him a place in a Cheshire Home. I was rude to the poor man when he obviously believed he'd done his best for James, snarling at him when he declared it was for the best. Yes, it was a solution but not a good one, not worthy of the obvious self-satisfaction displayed. James was back inside an institution however benign, aspects of his life regulated by others.

Another comrade whose story distressed me was an eighteen year old who had been working as a builder and suffered a mysterious problem with his elbow which was diagnosed as an elbow bleed only once the joint had been well and truly damaged. Blood tests had revealed the truth that he had haemophilia, presumably mild or moderate as he'd never undergone an internal bleed before, and luckily had needed no surgery or tooth extraction. The diagnosis had left him alternately depressed and filled with undifferentiated anger. Although my own journey had been so different, severe haemophilia announces its presence early and with irritating regularity, I found it easy to empathise with his dismay and rage. I assume that he would have been thrown out of work on insurance concerns.

The motor dealer who had suffered a brain haemorrhage and lived, the middle-aged clown who claimed that a bar of soap had slipped out of his hands in the bath causing a bleed that bent his penis (more likely Peyronie's Disease) Ian who wrote to me at home not to get a response as had others over the years, my strange reluctance to mix home with hospital the cause of such shameful behaviour, twin brothers one of whom worked at a university college and others added to my understanding and ability to see my fellow haemophiliacs as individuals first.

The opportunity to share stories of the good and bad treatment, acceptance and rejection common to most was invaluable to me. I often felt isolated, sometimes due to my own efforts and personality, and the opportunity to hear other members of what I took to calling haemophilia club recount how they coped or not was useful to me without changing anything in my own life.

As an adult that life was punctuated by extraordinary events and people, extraordinary to look back on but just part of my life at the time.

While I can count the amount of times I indulged in smoking weed on the fingers of one hand, the effect being that I found everything even more hilarious than ever, the absurdity of life enhanced, my one hit of psilocybin psychedelic mushrooms proved less than amusing.

We visited friends who used the things regularly and while Zoe refrained her husband and we two indulged in what I was assured was a moderate hit. That one of us chose to remain clear-headed was soon shown to be a sensible precaution.

The television was switched on as I was assured this could lead to interesting effects and we sat in front of it. The first thing I noticed however was the ceiling which writhed with patterns of intersecting lines. Then the TV intervened as a black loose limbed puppet of some kind lashed out with arms that reached out into the room. Shortly after this the revelations started.

It was revealed unto me that everyone in the world was connected in threes into an ever expanding grid of triangles and that this did not rely on individuals knowing the other two, the obvious connections being quite tenuous. Rod my fellow mushroom taker and, of all the possible people in the world, Peter Knowles a footballer with Wolverhampton Wanderers, nonsensical in retrospect but complete sense at the time were the other two members of my 'cell'. So amazing and stupid of me not to have known it before that I yelled 'Yes, I should have known!' and when Zoe asked me to tone it down this too seemed revelatory 'Yes, of course keep it to myself, yes, yes!' She again asked me to be quiet and 'Quiet I yelled that's the way, yes'. 'Please be quiet the nieghbours will be calling the police'. This seemed an amazing discovery, a world shaker and beside myself with joy having at last found the key that made sense of every aspect of universe I yelled all the louder. Zoe called a friend and Rod and Mike frog marched me to a car and drove me out into the deepest countryside to shout for as long as it took.

I think the word police caused the down turn in my state of mind and I misperceived the car as a military vehicle and Rob and Mike as state goons who took me to a desert and chopped me into pieces, scattering bits of me about (I'd been reading Egyptian mythology, Osiris strewn among the dunes) and it didn't appear strange to me that I could be misused on the one hand and be able to witness it on the other. Then the scene changed and I was an entity spewing out whole universes from my mouth, words but each word a cosmos (The Word?) and after that I became the centre of a wheel whose opposite spokes had voices giving opinions of me, the voices and opinions polar opposites. Clever/dunce, weak/strong, loyal/ traitorous, handsome/ugly and so on and the opposing voices grew louder and louder until I realised my task was to quiet them, willing them into silence with every last bit of my determination.

Chapter 19

It was too much of a strain to hold them quiet for long and gradually as my grip weakened they began to whisper, then talk then bellow once more until I regained control. I quickly found that imposing silence during the whispering phase involved much less effort.

Then I appeared to wake up on the backseat of the car head down in the foot well, I could see Rob and Mike in the front seats and knew it was them but their faces didn't exist, nothing there but blank skin. I knew the same thing didn't apply to me and that I'd somehow awoken in another reality where I was unknown. I told myself not to panic and if I only made sure no one recognised me as alien all would work out. That was more or less the end of the trip as my companions noticed me moving and shivering, my top-half was naked as they'd stripped me and walked me round and round the local reservoir to 'sober' me up and we drove back to my partner and Zoe.

A few months later Rod took his own life, I was shocked as I thought him stronger than that. Ex parachute regiment, I regarded him as tough minded but who knows what gory experiences may leave latent in the mind. It was reported to me that Zoe didn't want to see me as she couldn't face me. Why is still a mystery to me, did she think I blamed her? Did she unaccountably blame me? Within a few months she sold up and moved to Wales, having been given her address by a mutual friend I sent a card wishing her well and let her slip into the past as she obviously wished.

At an Outsiders event we met a woman notorious for running a brothel. She held regular parties at which sex was for hire rather than an open house with a set of whores to choose from. She invited us to a party, not as punters but for atmosphere. She had friends, not working girls, who had been her party guests for some years.

Her clientele were an interesting lot, obviously suffering from the weight of bloated wallets and recruited from the great and the good. The food and drink was plentiful and the preliminary exhibition amusing and stimulating after which couples left the room and disappeared upstairs at intervals. Madame herself ruled with a rod of iron, more accurately a riding crop although I only saw her wield it once holding it under the chin of one of the working girls while uttering only one word 'Don't'. As the business end of the evening started she raised the crop and ordered 'No peeing!' A transvestite waitress, black fishnet tights, ultra-short mini skirt and all served the drinks.

In the early hours we commandeered one of the bedrooms and slept, door locked to the chagrin of at least two couples who banged and shouted at the door.

Next morning as we ate breakfast Madame, staff of office the riding crop under her arm, ordered another who'd stayed the night to get on with his task of mowing the lawn with scissors. It turned out that this man was either a highly paid and respected lawyer or high court judge, opinions differed.

I still chuckle whenever I recall that after one of the police raids on the house in evidence a moronic copper revealed that he and his colleagues, to gain entrance, ' Dressed as bi-sexuals'. Writing of transvestites, we once knew a man who delighted in his fem persona.

I won't name the man or his chosen fem name; let's say I have forgotten both. He loved to visit us 'dressed' as we had no trouble accepting him as a woman, whereas most others were not so tolerant. I must stress here that he/she and we did not indulge in any sexual activity.

We quickly forgot her male persona and she felt able to relax more fully with us than she usually did when dressed. When fully in his male role he was a pathologist at a large Midlands hospital and joked that at least in his job he wasn't required to take work home. Our contact with him/her was brief owing to the briefness of our own journey as a gang of two.

Our encounter with a transsexual friend was not such a happy one. Male to female, which she carried off well enough when dressed, she suggested a threesome, the novelty factor being a clear incentive we made the arrangements. It did not go well.

It turned out she was also deeply into latex and liked to be whipped. She stood there covered in black latex the close fitting emphasizing the fact that her rump and legs were mannish and when she asked me to whip her I felt that she and I were foolish participants in a farce. Harder, she implored when I tried to use the whip, but this proved impossible, I would have had to be enraged with her or the world in general and neither anger nor the wish to simulate could I dredge up, unkindly leaving her need and expectation unfulfilled.

At that point Dora and I should have backed out but determination and curiosity won the day and then I lost all desire on seeing the unfortunate job surgery had done; no longer male or female in my eyes she took on the attributes of a person mauled into a strange form of disability. The emotions roused were anger towards the perpetrator and pity. The unfortunate thought stuck me that though female, concave where the male would be convex her species was a mystery. Her breasts were solid, the size of cricket balls and as hard, stuck onto a man's chest as incongruous add-ons and the vagina they'd constructed was nothing more than a hole under a bony bit of pelvis, the meatus of the penis retained and partly hidden behind a flap of skin with a smaller hole. No attempt had been made to render the mess vagina like. End of story.

I was introduced to one of Dora's old lovers, a man who had served time for GBH and other crimes, had boxed and wrestled professionally and could tell stories of his past, amusing or horrifying by turns. He used to joke that he was the only one amongst us who could prove sanity as he had a piece of paper that said so after a psychiatric assessment on being caught during one of his worst crimes. I could relate what he told me about various crimes and how authority had it all wrong and how he witnessed a murder but that might even now give too much away.

I hope the statute of limitations covers the only crime he and Dora both took part in but in any case I think I've obscured the facts quite well. Together they had broken a man out of prison using the corny but effective method of throwing a rope over the wall after which all three made off by car. They were never caught but what happened to the erstwhile convict and why it was imperative to get him out of his custodial predicament I have conveniently forgotten.

While the gratuitous violence Dora's old chum indulged in repelled me I remain grateful for having the chance to meet him and learn how yet another specimen of homo sapiens created his path through the world. In my own travail as revealed in three books, I've shared time with the conventionally good and bad the latter more memorable and the majority mostly forgettable. Circumstance ruled what my old acquaintance did or espoused and I have learned that I am capable of anything, good or bad as need or want prompts.

Though I knew only a few of them and much here will have been told to me or is the product of research, this is the place to write about my parent's aunts, uncles and cousins.

Dad had very little that was good to say about his mother's family, the Woods; he detested his maternal grandfather after being forced to help him with his gardening job and if he chose to disparage anyone in the family he would call he or she a Wood and his mother's siblings were the source of either amusement or scorn, mostly the latter.

Aunt Cad (Caroline) had a daughter Gladys, tall, slim and aloof on the only occasion I recall meeting her and, presumably, a husband of whom I know nothing; she also owned a large wen or fatty cyst on her cheek and a cackling laugh. She was mostly harmless apart from when at the point of my departure she would demand a kiss on the cheek, presenting the disfigured one and letting out a cackle as I turned my head away. I once visited her home when quite young and was impressed by a conservatory or veranda, anyway something comprising metal and glass and the contents of this short paragraph are my only memories of her. I have since learned that Gladys always referred to as Glad was profoundly deaf and this accounts for the aloofness I found as a child. The two were lumped together in conversation as Cad and Glad!

Aunt Em (Emily) always spoken of as though worthy of capital letters as The Aunt Em, a widow living in a large detached house in a posh area of the city was plump from good living, had white permed hair and a blustering sense of her own importance.

When a member of the family married, the reception was held at her home and the youngest there were my cousin Robin and me. The garden was huge, big enough anyway for her to offer to let us play with her deceased husband's bowls or putters and golf ball. We plumped for golf and she warned us not to whack at the ball but just to putt. Almost immediately Robin swung hard at the ball and it flew over the fence into the next door garden. To do him justice Robin went to report to The Aunt Em and she came out furiously calling to me: Derek, I told you not to hit the ball so hard! Such an injustice, I held my tongue, the dignified response to mistaken accusation I'd learned to adopt by then, she might be 'The hag with the money' but I was equally self – important, at least to myself and could outlast her and take my revenge if it ever became possible and if I still felt it to be worth my while.

Chapter 20

The Aunt Em and her husband Dickie (Herbert) Pemberton and a partner had made money out of tobacco and sold the business on for a large sum of money. He had played Rugger for Coventry and my researches lead me to believe, is mentioned in a club publication as one of fifty 'greats' to have played for the club. Rugby football was viewed with contempt by my father and while he acknowledged that Pemberton had been an England schoolboy Rugby international averred that such were ten-a-penny.

My mother's attitude was not so contemptuous of either of the Pembertons; my feeling is that she thought Dickie was a gentleman and The Aunt merely foolish. She would mention a little wistfully that she'd been offered domestic work by them and Dad had blown up in anger and forbade it, as being symptomatic of an overweening attitude that saw his wife as suitable servant material and himself as a pauper worthy of support.

Fan (Frances) also had a daughter Maggie who I don't recall ever meeting and lived in a house with only one feature that impressed me, namely a large bell on the wall of the living – room. The bell was left over from the time when her husband had been a fireman and it had been rung from the fire station when he was needed. Aunt Fan was the most comfortable to know of Gran's sisters, shorter, rounder minus a teasing wen, and without the spurious authority that money confers.

She was the adherent of a faith, though exactly which I was always unsure of. Mum told me on different occasions that Fan was a spiritualist and a Pentecostalist. Perhaps I felt out of my depth as I never asked Fan about her beliefs, I know it would have interested me so this is puzzling. All I do know is that the practical outcome of knowing this great Aunt with the glasses whose demeanour showed a mixture of cheerfulness and concern was the laying on of hands! On the couple of times Mum took me to her house she knelt down and placed both hands on whichever knee joint had lately bled, bowed her head, closed her eyes and prayed in a barely audible tone more obvious from her lips moving than any recognisable words. A strong image of Fan standing at the foot of my hospital bed, head bowed after dark and smiling at me when she noticed I was awake before motioning me to be quiet and moving on to the next bed has been a part of my memory of her since childhood. Whether this actually happened, was a dream, a flight of fancy or astral projection (!?!) I am unable to differentiate.

The last memory of her is an unfortunate one; she suffered a stroke and after the initial treatment was transferred to some horrible geriatric hospital at Exhall. Perhaps this establishment was not as horrible as it appeared to me when we visited but the sight of the old people lined up in hospital style comfy chairs in a room redolent of stale urine appalled me. She reached out her one good arm and felt the cloth of my jacket and, being unable to speak, made a couple of shushing noises indicative of approbation. Seeing her so helpless, who had attempted to heal others, not able to heal herself and confined in a stinking pit was too much for me and I left for the open air, staying outside until my parents decided to go. What feelings did my desertion arouse?

Shame and self-disgust at having run from a reality that hurt and tormented me but despite this I stayed outside until my parents emerged and we left. I never said goodbye and only a little while later aunt Fan died. Whatever her beliefs I hope she found what she hoped to find and if only oblivion awaits the dead then she would have been oblivious.

Gran's brother Jack appeared to be quite humourless, this impression may be down to not being well acquainted with him however as we visited only infrequently when he was alive though spent much time with Dad's cousin Mary and her husband and daughter once he'd gone. He apparently predicted that once he died the small amount of money he left would be spent on a motor vehicle, he was right.

In hospital and suffering the illness from which he died, Jack had a visit from various members of the family including Gran and The Aunt Em. He was said not to know anyone so she pushed herself forward and announced that he would know her: I am Em, who am I? With a wink at Mum he responded 'How the hell should I know, if you don't.'

Fred Wood Gran's other brother I never met but was often told by Dad that he was a typical Wood by which he meant money obsessed and selfish. Other than this assessment of character all I know is that the man owned a farm, which he sold to buy a larger farm. This I was told by Gran.

My father's Haughton Aunts and uncles I have no recollection of meeting, and the little I know of them comes from a few anecdotes, one letter and details gleaned from various genealogical records.

Dad told me a story of the teatime habits of the members of one part of the extended family which embarrassed him and, as he put it, contributed to his hating to go and visit. The meal would be on the table and the kids warned to wait as the father sat with a raised tablespoon which he would bang down and say go! A free for all would ensue, boys and girls grabbing what they could. I often wonder if this was one of the first episodes to put my father off visiting the Haughton side of the family. A number of these people I never knew because they deceased before or shortly after my birth but sufficient remained plus cousins though we avoided them.

William, my grandfather's brother known as Billy – was Grandad's dog named after him? – was known in the family as Woodbine Willie; this detail lurked in the back of my mind until reminded by a story on a genealogy website. I met his son, my father's cousin, when we paid them a sudden visit, just the once, in my late teens. Why this happened I had no idea at the time but have speculated while writing this that Dad may have asked if Les could use whatever influence he had to get me a job where he worked. Pure speculation, why Dad took these notions to suddenly visit relations was part of the mysterious way he conducted himself.

Billy's wife Minn died in 1960 and in amongst my mother's papers I discovered a letter of thanks addressed to my parents and family my uncle and family and my gran Billy's sister-in-law who he addresses as Rose; not unexpected but strange to read as I always knew her as Gran. It would be wrong of me to reveal details of the brief note, suffice it to say he missed Minn tremendously and that I regret not knowing him.

Grandad's sister named Alice after her mother and known as Al, was the victim of only one story and I tell it as it was told to me by Dad: The whole family went to the circus and sat in the front row; the educated donkey was asked to 'Pick me out the woman as likes a drink on the sly!' and it selected aunt Al who simpered and blushed. The story amused me but the lady seemed too much of a character from history and the only other fact regarding her I knew was that her husband was Charlie Jones.

Another sister I know even less about; Winifred May married Tom (Alf? Dad often mentioned an Alf never a Tom) Harris producing one daughter, Betty Winifred who died unmarried and intestate in 1998.

A third sister, Amy married James Kettle and of her I know only that fact. Jim Kettle joined the army and fought in the First World War and, although sceptical of some of the details, this is what was told to me: The family made a joke of watching him march with his regiment equating Jim with the song written by Irving Berlin in 1917, They Were all Out of Step but Jim. More stirring, despite the family dislike of military matters, was the story that he progressed to sergeant-major in the Royal Field Artillery and was pictured in a newspaper of the time single-handedly manning a gun with his comrades lying dead or wounded around him. And for his heroism was mentioned in dispatches. These latter details I will try to verify but they may well be wishful thinking or unwitting misrepresentation.

Also living in Grandad's family was Frederick Mather who until recently I had assumed was my great grandmother's (Alice Prudence nee Mather) brother but during research into the family I now know to have been the son of her unmarried sister. On baptism no father was recorded. He also took part in the 1914-18 war but this time in a role more acceptable to the Haughton ethic, a stretcher bearer. Of his experiences in the trenches I know nothing or what he did after the war, indeed, the only mention of him was when Mum said apropos what I don't recall, that she liked Fred Mather, the only other person she liked in the family being Grandad this was high praise. Fred died before I was born.

My father and grandfather were both scathing in their view of the military and our Glorious Leaders in general, Dad referring to one member of the family as being recruited into the King's Loyal Standbacks and the Scouts having only one function, to produce cannon fodder.

Chapter 21

The Boys Brigade earned similar dismissal though found amusing because of the silly uniforms rather than being the proving ground for those uniformly obedient.

Here comes the Boys Brigade
all covered in marmalade
a tuppenny-hapenny-pill-box (referring to the headgear)
and half-a-yard o' braid.

I would be told of a member of the family who came back from the first war shell – shocked and who would tremble and tear strips of newspaper to block any gaps around doors and window frames as he relived the terror associated with mustard gas. Any sudden loud noise could lead to his slipping back into a state of panic and it took some time before the attacks first diminished and later ceased altogether.

Dad, if he heard the words they shall not grow old as we grow old on Remembrance Sunday, would assume his grim-faced look and respond with 'They would have liked the chance to'. Mum would give an expressive sniff of agreement, say yes and sigh. I would marvel, as I grew up, at the curious combination of deference to and contempt for authority and accepted tradition so often manifested in our home.

Royalty was either despised, excepting the abdicated King Edward, or viewed as absurdly comical and ostentatious money bags. The birth of another specimen greeted by Dad's 'Another mouth to feed!' Winston Churchill was a turncoat warmonger and no word in his defence was tolerated, Harold Macmillan and Alec Douglas-Home were domino teeth and skull-face respectively. Politicians of whatever hue, florid or apoplectic, were not well regarded in fact and those in-betweeners, the liberals spoken of as dead-but-they-won't-lie-down. A change of name and (2012) tory coat tails to cling to have seen a partial resurrection to zombie state but this does not negate my father's assertion.

It amused me to hear politicians opine that the expenses scandal of just a few years back had damaged the trust people had in politicians and politics in general as I vividly recall hearing many say during elections in my childhood: It don't matter who you vote for they're all the same, out to line their own pockets! Not that my parents promulgated the remark but they never protested it either.

On the other hand my father applauded expertise and learning, to be good at one's job earned his praise and he doted on those he found intelligent. He, and by extension we, never missed The Sky at Night, the television program fronted by Patrick Moore as he found the man erudite and convincing. Two others I recall from television's *The Brains Trust* were Jacob Bronowski, multi talented writer of The Assent of Man and Marghanita Laski, secular humanist, writer and journalist who when Mum interrupted would provoke Dad into telling her to listen as this was an intelligent woman the inference being that she might learn something. In retrospect the three broadcasters certainly stimulated with their well expressed opinions and explanations often alien to those around me and offered me more of an education than school ever did.

The aforementioned deference could be stimulated in my father by any challenge to medical personnel, solicitors or anyone whose education lifted them to a higher plane of existence, at least in his eyes but woe to him or her who assumed the mantle without just cause.

My father could be hypercritical of most people with very little cause at times, from the man who lived up the street and who organised a day-trip to the sea for locals and was thereafter referred to as the president of Sewall Highway to the unmarried couples exposed by perusal of the book mentioned earlier, possibly a bound copy of the electoral roll.

I've written elsewhere, chiefly in my autobiographical book What Are Yer? Bleeder!, a good deal about various cousins, aunts and uncles but left out one of Mum's sisters and my favourite Hamlet Uncle, her brother Fred.

Aunt May married John who she met through some kind of lonely hearts club, or so I was led to believe by parents who obviously found the information quietly amusing, giving it a mention whenever May and John came up in conversation, or were about to pay a very rare visit. I recall Aunt May as an entirely neutral entity, a sort of background hum even when present, and the antithesis to her sister Auntie Flo who laughed long and often, even a smile seemed forced and alien. I could be an obnoxious child, outspoken when children were expected to be seen and not heard, sharp tongued in self-defence, ever questioning received wisdom, it seems therefore, likely that mutual dislike or perhaps distrust kept our interaction to a minimum. Not that meeting the couple came about very often but I have no recollection of anything she might have said or done on the few times I met her.

John, on what may have been the only visit to our home, I caught leaning down with his face close to the action, poking a pencil at my budgie Joey. I'm not saying that he was trying to impale the bird but it wasn't exactly a safe thing to do and I told him to stop. Far from being put out on being ordered about by a child he did as he was told smiled vacantly and wandered off into another room. From that moment on my suspicion that he had what we would now call minor learning disability became a certainty.

The couple lived in Doncaster, which Aunt Flo with a laugh would always refer to as Donny and took their holidays at Scarborough or Bridlington but one year they unwontedly came to Lincolnshire while we were making what had become our annual pilgrimage and arrangements were made to meet at Sutton-On-Sea. We were staying at Orby once more at Ken Bunn's parent's home and the six of us, Ken, Frances – Mum's niece – their daughter Coral, my parents and me awaited the arrival of John and May with no interest whatsoever on the part of most, excepting Mum who was looking forward to seeing her sister. They hove into view leading on the one hand their substitute child Sally, a Corgi and on the other a shuffling caricature of an old man known only as Uncle. John's avuncular carbuncle was a complete unknown to the waiting audience. Incredibly red faced, obviously the consequence of a medical condition or being left out in the sun too long, rather than embarrassment, tongue-tied and shambling he later became a figure of fun recalled as Nunky. The consensus among our adult members when the four pilgrims had wandered back to their holiday home was that the unexpected Nunky had become valued as a potential source of increase once his florid hue turned pale as all movement ceased and the will was read. Unfair perhaps but the adults in my past must never be maligned by the suggestion that they were fair in their assessments of character or motive. That's right, me neither....

Coral's father Ken Bunn died in horrifying circumstances when, having left farming he worked as a commercial vehicle driver. While checking the load in a lay-by he was hit by another articulated truck and was burned in the subsequent fire. Almost unrecognisable I can only hope that death came before he burnt. I still miss his cheerful expression and ready laugh whenever he visited.

Aunt Flo never married and Mum told me it was because she had seen too much of the horrors of the married state, but she was not prepared to elaborate. She was a favourite of mine because of her sense of fun not evident from her views on marriage but looking at old photographs I see her, in many of them, in typical pose head thrown back and laughing. This is not to suggest the lack of a serious, caring side but to point to the fact that laughter was never far away when with her. Of my mother's family she adhered to the Salvation Army to the end, having a strong faith and commitment.

Children loved her and as a child I looked forward to seeing her when others either repelled me or aroused no feeling whatsoever. She lived with and looked after her friend Edie who over the years I knew her became bedridden with severe arthritis. To take care of someone in such a position for a few weeks is not easy; to do the same for much longer draining, but although I never witnessed Aunt Flo's efforts I believe she would have been a cheerful and compassionate nurse. When Edie died she left me the complete works of Dickens for which I remain grateful.

Aunt Flo once accompanied us to Weymouth for a week's holiday spent in a flat quite near the sea and one sunny day we spent a whole afternoon together, just the two of us walking, talking, looking at this and that and laughing. Eventually she suggested we eat: I'm tired and feeling hungry, it's time to find a rest-your-aunt. And head back she laughed and I laughed with her.

Next day we drove on to Portland up a very steep hill as one of a long line of traffic which ground to a halt and after a few seconds the commercial vehicle to our front began to roll back towards us. Aunt Flo panicking leant forward and raising her hand palm first sternly told the van, Go Back! Go Back! As her advice was taken and the lorry moved forward she sat back laughing at her own initial fear and attempted intervention, especially I believe as it might be said to have worked.

I assume we went on to picnic but my strongest memory is of aunt Flo's Canute-like feat of commanding the traffic to go back, where he failed she triumphed. We looked at the chapel the Portland Prison inmates had built and Dad recounted for the first but not the last time how years previously on a visit, when the prison was still in use, he'd been asked by a convict breaking stones for cigarettes, 'Chuck us some fags mate?' in a raucous whisper and he'd thrown over the wall and down to the prisoner fifteen feet below a packet with several cigarettes, only to be harangued by a prison officer and threatened as to his future conduct.

Two further memories of that holiday when I must have been around twelve years are all that remain.

Chapter 22

On the shore I caught several small hermit crabs and formed the idea of keeping them in a salt water aquarium once home, they immediately died, yet another incidence of the well meaning incompetence of an interested but essentially ignorant attendee of special school. Our holiday flat was on the first floor and a window at the end of the corridor had fixed below it a rolled up rope ladder with wooden treads, in case of fire the window was to be opened and the rope ladder pushed out. Far from reassuring me that everything had been done that could be done to save us from premature cremation I wondered just how prone to catching fire the flats were and doubted my ability to climb down if it became necessary. Walking up and down stairs was difficult enough with my ravaged knees.

On Edie's death Aunt Flo moved into a one bedroom, first floor flat with a garden shared by the ground floor flat. I still have her gardening scissors passed on to me by my mother when Flo died. Before that sad event she lived in her flat for a good number of years, venturing to Norway as the guest of her erstwhile Salvation Army officer and his wife. She told me of the family's children exclaiming in astonishment Auntie Flo doesn't eat smor (closest rendition of Norwegian for butter without an o with a diagonal) finishing the story with her trademark laugh. Certain foods were omitted from her diet owing to an abdominal problem for which she'd had an operation many years before; butter perhaps was one of these.

When young I misunderstood the nature of the medical problem and the operation to correct it as it was made mysterious by Mum telling me I mustn't mention it and yet talking to others while keeping the details from me. It's more than likely that she didn't know the details herself. I thought at the time, being quite young, that her circumspection was due to not wanting to talk about some peculiarity of the female form unknown to me. An indication of the truth is that she always puzzled me by her assertion that Grandad died of an extended heart when, on obtaining a copy of his death certificate I deduced that she had misheard or read the words dilated cardiomyopathy associated with the chronic myocarditis mentioned though how why and by whose agency I have no idea. I'd never been comfortable with the idea of a heart that could extend but in my arrogant way I blamed the G. P. who signed the certificate for carelessness. Extended, where to, how far and what did it displace, and how had it led to death? Mum's vague mutterings about Aunt Flo's operation were vague because her understanding both of anatomy, medical terminology and words in general was poor.

Aunt Flo's flat having only one bedroom she acquired an armchair that reclined to form a single bed, kept in the lounge it meant relatives could visit and use the bedroom while she slept on the chair, thus it was that John and May came to stay for a week. Someone had bought Flo a cuckoo- clock which stimulated John's erratic interest and he inadvertently instigated an incident hilarious to me at the time so that even now many years later I'm chuckling at the memory.

Being thwarting in his efforts to examine my budgie, the imaginatively named Joey, with his pencil John was determined to use the instrument to examine the innards of the timepiece and its cuckoo nestling behind the little wooden doors, his intervention proved detrimental to the well being of the cuckoo and the strain caused it to lose its voice, or more accurately part of it. Thereafter the poor thing greeted the hours and quarters with a series of oos having lost its cuck.

So, on visiting Aunt Flo we would be assailed by an oo at every quarter and a flurry of repeated oos at say six o'clock. On the first visit after John's interfering with the clock by pencil power the oos were explained and Mum and Flo went downstairs to see the lady in the lower flat. Dad sat reading the local newspaper, a publication devoid of any interesting stuff unless you lived in the town but less boring than talking to me. For a while I sat doing nothing but hoping something might occur and wishing I had been invited to look at the garden. Half past three and the cuckoo called oo, Dad downs the paper, gets up, walks to the top of the stairs and shouts, the door being ajar, 'She's not here! She'll be back soon.' Cocks an ear for a moment and then picks up the paper and sits back down. I get the picture, and await the next oo with suppressed joy and anxiety in case the game is spoiled by the return of Mum and Aunt. Ten minutes, five minutes, a minute to go, then oo and out of the chair he jumps, the newspaper scattering to the floor, rushes back to the stairs and calls down that she's not back yet and hesitates before coming back into the room extremely agitated to ask me and the fates 'Where the hell are they?' then gathers up the pages of the paper and rearranges them with trembling hands. I settle back, expecting fun even if they return in time, at least I'll be able to listen to him as he breaks the news that someone has been calling for her. But better than distant church bells across field and copse four o'clock arrives with oo, oo, oo, oo, and 'Oh bloody hell!' wild eyed he makes for the stairs on unsteady legs ready to confront the oo calling woman who has now become desperate for admittance so as to gaze on the visage of auntie. At that point my compassion, such as it is, kicks in and I forgo the pleasure of watching him go downstairs, after all I don't want him to make a total fool of himself in front of me and I tell him it's the clock.

He's relieved but doesn't fully understand how far he's been misled because he tells Flo on her eventual return that someone's been calling for her. As I'd hoped this leads to more fun for me as both ladies are non-plussed and Mum asks why he didn't tell the person where Flo was or at least find out what the elusive oo merchant wanted and her name. I've told you, it was some woman, to which Mum gives her traditional reply what a funny man, adding as you will by now expect that it is the fault of his mother.

Fred, Flo and Mum's brother lived further along the avenue and often called round, on a couple of occasions his visit coincided with ours. He is the only one of Mum's brothers I met as a youngster but he was one of my favourite uncles. He once gave me a houseplant, some sort of trailer with little white flowers and in the Spring a tiny bulb pushed through the compost and opened, a miniature jonquil, heavily scented so that in the morning when the curtains were opened a burst of beautiful fragrance filled the room.

He'd led an interesting life and told me how he'd once lived in a converted railway carriage and had worked as a gardener and latterly a school caretaker where, he informed me, the little devils called him Freddy the Frog which he didn't mind. He also told me how he walked all the way to Yorkshire after a farm job that had been advertised and when he got there the farmer met him at the gate and told him the job had been taken the week before. When Fred remonstrated that he should have been informed the farmer pulled out the gate post and threatened to beat him over the head. I must have looked incredulous as he told me 'It's right, walked all that way just for that'.

Fred and his wife had a boy Roger living with them but when I referred to him as Fred's son Mum said no and that he was one Fred took to. She wouldn't maybe couldn't elaborate and suspecting a family secret I didn't ask but played with the amusing idea of Fred and wife walking down the street seeing a child and deciding to acquire him because they had 'quite taken to him'.

As Fred aged his health began to fail and he developed a stubborn leg ulcer that caused a loss of mobility. My second wife and I would visit him now and then but gradually he began to accuse people of stealing from him, nothing significant and often bizarre. 'Do you know who's been to see me? That sample from Barwell' sample being his mild derogatory term that I found delightful never having heard the word utilised in that way before. 'The so and so came the other day and stole my toilet roll! Asked for the toilet before leaving and when I went in there later she'd taken the new one and left an almost used up one in its place'. To say this seemed unlikely is an understatement and even more unlikely the tale he told next time we called concerning a new razor blade also purloined and replaced with an old one.

He also recounted how he'd mistakenly drunk what turned out not to be a cup of water. 'Oh, I was bad after that.' not surprising as the 'water' had in fact been diluted bleach! Other mysterious tricks and roguery were reported each time we visited and accusations made until I began to wonder if I too might be blamed and referred to as that sample from Coventry. Poor Fred, it seems obvious that his memory was going tricking him into apportioning blame where none existed. It shames me to say it but this and a silly incident reported to me was enough to encourage me to stay away. I preferred to think of him as the uncle who, in my teens, sent via my parents the houseplant with a jonquil bulb hidden in the compost.

Chapter 23

Someone gave my parents the gift of a miniature bottle of Drambuie which, never opened, sat for years incongruously on the dressing table in their bedroom. It occurred to me that this was unfortunate and a case of hoarding or more exactly because they would never have imbibed the stuff 'dog in the manger' so deciding to help them and myself I carefully opened it, drank the contents, filled the bottle with water and placed it back. I felt a glow of satisfaction at my selfless act and a further glow as the alcohol warmed me. The deed was never discovered and I wonder what happened to the bottled water when my parents, long after I had left home, moved to Cornwall, did they give it to someone, if so did that person drink and find Drambuie much overrated? I can only enjoy the speculation that it was so.

As if the loss of two infants and dealing with a stubborn and self-protective haemophiliac child, with disapprobation from her spouse's family were not enough to endure by a woman orphaned in her early teens she found herself kept short of money by a husband unduly influenced – as she would often remark – by his mother's insistence that the pittance proffered was quite sufficient and that she was a bad manager.

The after war austerity and rationing which continued well into my childhood lingered on in our household and compared to friends and neighbours our way of life seemed mean. So poor that Mum evolved schemes for finding extra cash.

Puzzled as I was by the scarcity of various items, comestibles – fruit and biscuits for instance – and those necessities taken for granted by other families, I never blamed Mum, being witness to her heroic efforts to balance the books without adequate resources. A sum of money was allocated to her each week out of which gas, electricity, rent and later mortgage, coal and the weekly shop all had to be paid, and she would sit with notebook, pencil and worried frown jotting down the weekly sums. Occasionally she would be in tears and I would try to help. Her planning I criticised until I got her to make a list of what had to be paid out weekly and it worked out to slightly more than she received from Dad. To quote Dickens' Micawber: result misery.

She would explain that she had to rob Peter to pay Paul and this was no solution, merely deferring the inevitable shortfall and its consequences. The extra money that enabled the fending off of disaster was generated by her resolute efforts alone.

As a member of the Co -Op Mum had a membership number, 50523, and this I learned at a tender age by hearing it repeated as every payment at the till would require her to quote the number and once a year a dividend would be paid. A dividend book would be taken to the Co-Op offices in town and the calculated return paid out. She supplemented her income by queuing and collecting not only hers but friends' and nieghbours' who hadn't the time or inclination to queue themselves, she would be given at least half-a-crown often five shillings by each of them.

Making new collars for the work shirts of other women's husbands using her sewing machine was another earner. She would unpick the old frayed collar, use it as a pattern and cut a piece of the shirt tail for the material for the new collar and then reassemble. I believe unknown to my father she once took on housework for a family member of the Coopers who often helped her out but I could never understand why this had to be or why we had to use cast off towels from the same source when by now Dad was a company director and why such exotica as an ironing board and a working clothes iron were not bought in the first case and replaced in the second. The ancient, broken electric iron was placed on the hotplate of the electric cooker until up to temperature and replaced again and again until the ironing was finished. The cooker itself was not in first class order as the temperature gauge on the front was broken and even more skill was needed in cooking on the thing, perhaps accounting for Mum's reputation as a poor cook? Bad manager *and* poor cook with a 'funny man' as a husband and a haemophilic son obdurate or bleeding, it must have been her own fault……

She looked forward to the electricity and gas metres being read, when all the shillings would be counted out into piles of one pound each and anything over the actual cost would be left on the kitchen table as rebate. The gas generating very little as gas was used only to power the copper on wash day and the geyser over the bath. Even so a little rebate accrued but the electricity metre reader was the more eagerly awaited.

Remember when crisps had a small bag of salt included in every packet back when the only flavour was salty potato? A firm canvassed for home workers to fill the little packets of salt and Mum was one of the women who took on the work and I helped though less than five years. little squares of shiny blue paper and a supply of salt were handed out and many families worked away, sadly no pay was handed out and the project folded the first scam I ever knew of.

Early memories of visits to the Co-Op include a bombsite on the opposite corner where a greengrocery van was parked, vegetables set out and always a queue of customers which in retrospect is odd as it was a curious place to sell vegetables being opposite the Co-Op greengrocery section. The van was not patronised by Mum who would have lost the potential 'divi', this I was grateful for as I appreciated the chute down which came the potatoes to replenish the wooden trays as customers emptied them. When very young I surmised that slaves were kept busy pouring down spuds as necessary but later noticed inverted sacks and gravity working the trick. Another favourite of mine was the large wooden box on castors that lived in the grocery section at the end of the large building, this contained sugar and a junior member of staff would scoop it into stiff blue paper bags, expertly folding the tops tightly closed. This achieved the resulting bags would be placed ready for sale. The box or trolley had a delicious, to me at least, burnt sugar smell. Once home with our groceries Mum would empty our bag of sugar into a tin and then run her hand round inside the bag and empty out a couple of tea spoons full that had adhered with the words waste not want not.

It must not be thought that Mum was continually unhappy she had friends who she talked and laughed with and many acquaintances and if out with her anywhere but especially on buses she spent most of the time chatting. That being said, when my mother squatted, gazing into the coal fire and absentmindedly drew a little face with her cigarette end on the black metal surrounding the grate, a row of dots for a mouth, two others close together for a nose and two more for eyes and then rose with a sigh, I knew she was thinking of her lost children and other dead. She knew something was amiss when in the night she dreamed all the family, living or dead were gathered round her bed, usually this presaged a death. This she claimed and I have no reason to doubt her. She had several sayings often repeated when deemed necessary: If things don't alter they'll stay as they are! There's a good many mites in a pound of cheese (when someone said they might) and the vulgar: ah well said the soul, ah soul said the well. These will do as a sample.

One Christmas morning, the neighbourhood alive with merry greetings and seasonal good cheer, Mum was enticed into a neighbour's house for a celebratory drink and on emerging from their home was hailed by other neighbours and felt obliged to drink what was offered, three tipples in a morning imbibed by a woman who would give a comical shudder whenever she sipped an alcoholic drink. I don't think this was meant to be comical but more of an indication of reluctance such as a child might indulge in to indicate the awful nature of having to take something good for her but an imposition. The outcome was that when she tried to carry a stack of plates from the larder to the table they slipped from her fingers and there she stood the fruits of her debauchery in pieces at her feet, ten times as wary of the demon drink as before. The episode was never forgotten.

By the time my memories of my mother start she had given way to temptation and forgone her Salvation Army principles although she only ever wore a little in the way of make-up, occasionally face powder and lipstick and her alcohol intake was at most minimal she smoked, both parents did and although I have no memory of it impinging on me when very young later it was a real nuisance as I sat in the back of the car on a cold winter night

Chapter 24

With the windows closed and the pair smoking away. My eyes would stream and I would beg them to open the window for a while and although they would comply I had to listen to what I already knew, it would be cold. In a couple of minutes the air would clear and then up would go the window again until the next cigarettes, smokers never smoke alone, rendered the atmosphere barely breathable and the process would be repeated. If we'd known about the dangers of passive smoking back then I would have been angry as they would have found.

It must have been Dad who introduced her to the benefits of booze but it was family friend Vi who persuaded her to use make-up telling her she could look lovely if she tried and reading between the lines it would not be surprising if Dad's ardour had faded a little, after all virginity and a pure nature that abhorred swearing, booze, cigarettes and self-adornment are all very well as attractants to a certain kind of man but virginity doesn't survive the wedding night, if that long and for a man who smoked and drank, often to excess, Mum's reticence must certainly have had the clammy feel of the wet blanket and the restriction of the strait jacket. The smoking came as a prescription to settle Mum's nerves from the same source as the innocuous make-up but the nicotine fix the cause of eventual misery.

Both parent's deaths were hastened by nicotine addiction, the relentless cigarette smoking contributing significantly to both the sudden coronary infarct suffered by Dad and Mum's vascular dementia.

Kippering others, both lungs and clothing, running to replenish stocks, ensuring that one has a light and spending the last of your wages on poisonous ephemera, is legal but as miserable a life as that of any other addict.

My mother had abandoned her early Salvation Army principles by allowing herself to be persuaded that smoking would 'settle her nerves', throughout my childhood a better support for my mother's nerves was the collaboration, to our joint benefit, with Mr Harry Parry-Williams, paediatric surgeon, a caring and highly competent practitioner. Friendly and understanding he knew that the well being of his young patients was best served by cooperation between all parties. I would like to claim that he was my confidant but alas within a few short years I had learned not to put that amount of trust in any adult. The fact that I felt physically safe in his team's care in spite of my less than trustful nature must be taken as an indication of this patient's regard.

He saved me pain, protected me from orthopaedics as much as possible and prolonged my life from infancy to late teens. Prolonged my life, not saved. I profess to write, not well and not profusely, poetry (note: I do not claim to be a poet) and all such writers know that lives are not saved but prolonged, death being the inevitable outcome of living.

Protected me from orthopaedics, is disingenuous, he protected me from Mr Bizzaro, surgeon, whose method of dealing with children was old fashioned, stand-offish and to an extent brutal. To be fair to the man however his constant application of full leg plaster or leg braces may, after all, have been one of the reasons my bleed ravaged knees lasted as long as they did, finally giving out in my fifties.

To resume eulogising Harry Parry; he supported me and cared for me with humour and genuine compassion, as he did so many other children during his years as Coventry's Mr Paediatrics, and was sorely missed on his retirement. His patients collected money and bought him a comfortable reclining chair which regrettably he did not live to enjoy for long.

I have never forgotten his joining the cast in the middle of the chorus line for the finale of the Christmas pantomime, an annual event put on by the staff in the lecture theatre attached to the Nurses Home at my favourite hospital. I'd been an in-patient at all five Coventry hospitals and although being in hospital was not the best experience if it had to be then let it be Gulson Road. There he was arm in arm with delightful nurses, kicking his legs in time with them as the cast sang a version of McNamara's Band, changing the words to, Henessey, Tenessey Gulson Road.

Twice I spent Christmas in the hospital and attended the panto where both times he appeared as Father Christmas but only once joined in with the chorus line. The copious references to Ireland came from the fact that most of the nurses were recruited from there, a new intake of girls for training arriving each year.

Sometimes on meeting we would exchange frowns then he would raise his eyebrows, head back and the mutual frowns would change to smiles, his supposed infringement of my rules banning interference in my affairs forgotten and his invariable understanding of my transgressions to the fore. Once when I was ill in sick bay at Corley Open Air School he unexpectedly visited me, bringing with him W. S. Chinn head of education. I snatched up my trusty six shooter and picked them off as they came through the door. Bang, bang! Chinn, a Quaker just looked worried but old Harry Parry played the game and staggered clutching at his chest, laughed and walked on. This was not good enough for the little boy with the toy gun: Lie down, you bugger, you're dead. Consternation from Chinn as Harry P fell to the floor with a realistic groan to lie still for a few seconds to resurrect when we shared a laugh while Chinn looked on perplexed.

The last time I saw Harry P I was eighteen years old, not long out of my educational non-experience and walking down the corridor close to his clinic. He did a double take, staggered to the wall, steadied himself and awaited my approach, you will have gathered that he was a ham actor always ready for fun but very serious when required. What he said to me on this occasion had a huge impact on my future life: Are you aware of how well you've done to be walking at all, never mind as well as you are? With so many episodes of serious bleeding into those knees you should be using a wheelchair by now, please remember what I'm going to tell you and remember that I tell you this because I know you very well. Before you reach thirty you *will* be using a wheelchair to get around. I was stunned. We parted and I never saw him again.

I determined to prove him wrong, he said thirty I'd make it sixty and he would be one hundred per cent out in his prediction if it killed me.

Only in my mid-fifties was I forced to give in and use a chair, not because the knees had failed altogether but I needed a hip replacement which was stupidly delayed and the muscles I'd conscientiously conserved lost tone and that is when the knees gave up. The failure hit me hard, determination and intensive work were not enough and I'm not ashamed to say I cried tears of frustration until the obvious truth hit me and the tears turned to tears of gratitude and sadness that I'd not been able to confide in one of the greatest men I ever met.

Mr Harry Parry-Williams had gone on even after his death to do his best for me; he had indeed known me very well and knew I would drive hard to disprove his prognosis.

I could and perhaps should mention all the staff medical and surgical who have cared for me so well, many becoming friends, throughout my life in Oxford, Coventry and Birmingham but to do each one justice would double the size of this book and so I must content myself with saying thank you to all!

My brother Syd bore the brunt of my hero worship as a young child but this phase didn't last long as told in a previous book, What Are Yer? Bleeder! The depth of my feeling for him is perhaps not so obvious in that book, or perhaps it is, my self-serving advice is to read it. One Easter Sunday before my three years away at residential school, I sneaked into his room and sat on the dressing table eating his chocolates and dropping the little brown paper cups out of the window, trying to get them to land in the open topped rainwater butt while he was distracted by the radio. After three or four he gave a yell and came running upstairs and into the bedroom but didn't seem particularly put out and later told the story and laughed.

His tolerance should have given me a pointer as to my behaviour and taught me not to set my teeth at every slight and to keep a hold on the temper it took me in fact years to tame, but I proved impervious. He did however teach by example as when he and I were alone in the house he would lie back in an easy chair and put his feet up on the mantel shelf, but as Mum and Dad approached down came his feet and he would sit up straight. Thus he reinforced my own findings that you could do just as you wished as long as no one in a position of authority caught you.

He came limping in one day after an accident with his push bike. The road that led to church hill had never been made up although the houses had been finished just before the war when building had to stop and was just a jumble of large granite rocks, curiously similar to those surrounding a flower bed in our back garden. Householders had thrown down ashes and such in an attempt to make the road somewhat passable and to fill in the spaces where rocks had been purloined. This was some years after the war had finished. He chose to ride his bike through and around these obstacles inevitably hitting a large rock and going over the handle bars.

Chapter 25

In came Syd bent over and limping to sit down and tell me about it. My sympathy, if any, soon evaporated and I asked him what he would do if he were out in the country and a bull charged at him, and then I charged at him, he was up and running immediately and round and round the dining table we went. Full of aches and pains he didn't hold back and joined me in fun and that's how I remember him back then before I started school, my brother my hero.

Syd finished his national service imposition with REME and married Violet Atkins before I returned from my three years at residential school. The couple had visited me at Corley and also in Gulson Road hospital and I liked Vi. Instructed to regard her as my sister I had no difficulty with that and she was always very kind and showed sympathy to a little boy often in pain during the visits. My parent's attitude to their daughter-in-law was blighted by doubt from the first which quickly turned to the usual dismissive criticism rife within my immediate family, where even the mildest of transgressions might be picked on and over for months.

Dad would frequently drag out what became an old chestnut of a complaint concerning Syd's not taking the opportunity to learn a proper trade during national service, with a tut and a jerk of the chin he'd reiterate his disgust: working in the stores, no trade at all. While Mum would recount back to him once again the story of Vi's blunder, on first coming to tea, telling a risqué joke to her potential in-laws, and repeating his comment once alone with Mum the ironic: bloody hell, she's a bright spark! Poor Vi was probably nervous and tried a witticism to break the ice, as she told me later she really had no idea that a double entendre was what made the remark a joke. Here are the words that earned the long term disapprobation. Question: Why didn't the blonde cross the road? Answer: Because the policeman had his hand up!

The newly-weds moved in with Vi's parents, and had the use of a downstairs room which soon they shared with their first born, my niece when I became an uncle at only nine years old. The room must have been crowded with a double bed and a cot but the house seemed crowded to me anyway, Mr and Mrs Atkins, Syd and Vi, I believe Vi's sister and a lodger Trevor. A later addition was a kitten supposedly bought for the child and named Korky after the perceived similarity of markings to Korky the Cat on the front cover of the comic Dandy. In the circumstances the acquisition of a pet was the last thing that was needed and the first of many unfortunate mistakes.

I liked Mrs Atkins but didn't take to the miserable Mr Atkins whose ill-mannered demeanour and permanent looks of disapproval could quickly chill the jolliest of gatherings. I never saw the man smile, still perhaps he felt he had nothing to smile about. What he thought of his daughter and son –in- law and their efforts to raise a child in difficult circumstances and doing the best they could in spite of interference from my parents and early on Mrs Atkins, I don't know.

I tended to blame Mum and Mrs Atkins for the continual harassment by good advice that marred the young marriage but later came to realise that Dad, as so often in the future, stoked the fire of Mum's disapproval while keeping out of the fray himself. The information that drew the flack could only have come from Mrs Atkins but the yapping and complaining was shared between the three. The baby was allowed to sleep with her parents and wasn't put to bed at a reasonable time and the young family didn't get up at a reasonable time in the morning and were said, as categorised by my father, to 'lie stinking in bed'. A plan was hatched and Mum went to the Atkins' to catch the couple in bed one morning at an hour when she supposed reasonably competent parents ought to be up and about for the welfare of the child.

They were indeed still in bed and my mother triumphantly claimed to have thumped on their door and 'got them out'. I expect both were resentful of the rude awakening and the collusion between parents that this implied. What Mr Atkins thought of the proceedings wasn't mentioned, or his opinion of my brother, but our own father remained critical of Syd and of Vi for the rest of his life and I would feel indignant on their behalf, it was after all their business how they accomplished their domestic arrangements and the direction of their marital accommodations, as it had also been up to Syd to decide on his career or lack of it.

The young family moved house to a ground floor maisonette, fascinating to me because of the construction, a couple of rooms then stairs up to the bedrooms with another household perched on top. Over the course of a few short years the terraced blocks came to be perceived as a den of thieves and a dumping ground for problem families but at the time they moved in no one suspected such a downturn. The blocks were new and no doubt it came as a relief to be left in peace and to have the space to move around without tripping over so many feet. The cat, Korky, did not accompany them.

Two further children were added, P and L and needing a three bed-roomed house the family moved to a semi in a different part of the city, but before that I enjoyed an occasional weekend stay, of which I remember very little apart from how welcome I was made to feel and the delight I took in my niece. The characters who visited them, neighbours who came to borrow and one or two friends I found mildly dubious to say the least. Living with my parents had honed my own hypercritical sensibilities not to snobbery as Mum said of me: What's he got to be snobbish about? on hearing me accused but I admit to preferring to keep my distance and wracked by embarrassed distaste, unless of course I've just given a wordy description of a snob? I was often amused by what was said and done around me but would also often cringe instead.

I have a photograph of an outdoor children's party held at the back of the maisonettes, possibly a birthday, possibly my niece's. All the neighbourhood children were there, me too with Mum who was helping Vi, and one of the little girls was of Caribbean extraction and very dark skinned. Mum was very taken with her and said: Oooh, isn't she lovely, I always wanted a black doll! What I wanted was to be anywhere but there, cringe is not the word and embarrassed doesn't cover it, I couldn't forget it for long enough to enjoy the rest of the party and every time the thought obtruded I wished I could erase Mum, me or both.

On entering Syd's place on another day I found him busily polishing away at light bulbs with a piece of emery cloth, a curious procedure which he explained to his own satisfaction but dismay on my part. The bulbs carried the words Property of Coventry City Council which he was spending time and effort on removing.

The outside staircases and walkways for the upper tier were meant to be lit for the safety of all and these bulbs were regularly purloined from thence on the council replacing them. Replacement was frequent on complaints from residents and the bulbs would immediately go missing once more. As he only had a couple I suspected one of the dubious had passed them on to him. Noticing my incredulous look he told me that everyone took the bulbs. This I could believe but how many of them bothered to waste their time scrubbing away at the things in case authority raided the home to check the light fittings for stolen goods I wondered. Too mean to buy a couple of light bulbs and too liable to disable precautions meant for their own benefit that was my assessment. I tried valiantly to exclude my brother from the general malaise but knew I was fooling myself. The mean and idle stole from each other indiscriminately anyway. A hire purchase television could be stolen from one flat make its way gradually along the block and be offered back at a knock down price to the original owner a few weeks later or so it was said.

Not unexpectedly the family suffered a break in and this time I agreed as Dad said, it was their own fault. In those days if you chose to go down a foolish route you could have a cigarette machine installed in your home. I suppose it provided some sort of discount amounting to extra income, an unsound idea if tempting. Tempted, the machine was fixed to the wall in the living room and several times a day the dubious and sometimes grubby neighbours would knock and be allowed in to service their nicotine addiction.

What a surprise, someone forced the door in the night, broke open the machine taking money and cigarettes and curiously a two pound bag of sugar from the kitchen. Presumably the culprit was a friend who attacked the ciggy machine as an afterthought when they forced the door not wanting to awaken the family in the night while desperate to borrow a cup of sugar!

Another foolish act of my brother provided a talking, or whining point for many years after the event.

Chapter 26

Syd stood as guarantor for a rogue who bought, on terms, a push-bike from a local shop. Inevitably the dubious one failed to pay and Syd was stuck with the bill. He didn't have the money, and told our mother who told our father, who predictably went red in the face and asked the universe and Mum why Syd had done something so idiotic, that he'd been told never to stand guarantor and why did he have to crawl to his mother and get her to beg Dad to fix the problem. And, embarrassing for me fourteen years the younger brother, why couldn't he be more like Derek who if he has a need speaks directly to his father. My parents went to see the shop keeper and what the details of the interview were I never found out apart from hearing Mum say that the man had apologised for the tone of his letter and the precipitate nature of his attempt to get recompense. He had thought my brother was like the rest of them round there.

The three of us and presumably Syd and Vi too were pleased to have them leave the notorious blocks behind in Willenhall and move to a semi -detached three-bedroomed house in Canley in a neighbourhood generally viewed as reasonably civilised. It must not be thought that there was now less to carp and complain about regarding Syd and Vi and their chosen way of surviving married bliss.

Dad would say, as if this hadn't been rehearsed enough all week, on the car journey to Canley: I hope he's not doing the ironing again, he wants to tell her to get off her fat arse and do a bit. And I hope the place isn't full of riff-raff, he should have learned that lesson by now. Mum would agree and in the back of the car I'd squirm knowing what was being set up. Sure enough, on arrival Syd would be ironing or if not cleaning, or cooking and Vi would be sitting on her posterior which was not in fact enormous but did have a tail which she'd asked if I would like to feel through her clothing, I imagine I took her word for it. The fact was something to keep quiet about as if mentioned to Dad he would have said he wasn't at all surprised. On arrival Dad would keep his mouth shut, smiling away at his grand-children while Mum commented on his ironing again or asked Vi what the matter was and if she'd hurt her leg. The whole thing sickened me, how I wished she would tell Dad to speak up if he had anything to say not complain to her and then sit there smiling benevolence with not even the grace to look sheepish. So Syd didn't speak to him but went to his mother did he? Didn't Dad do the same thing, why not talk to his son, in private if need be?

With hindsight I wonder if Syd got a thrill out of being humiliated, certainly the way he lived would indicate that he did? Mum reminded him in my presence on more than one occasion that when he'd committed some minor offense, cheekiness or some such, when he was fourteen years old, she had put him across her knee and spanked his bare bottom, not a good way to treat an adolescent boy! I resist speculation or interpretation of motives, or actions suffered and initiated during those long gone years, suffice it to say that now all the adult protagonists are dead, the futility of constant criticism and the inability to empathise are all too evident. A happier situation could have existed if the need to control and the fear of offspring not living up to one's own faulty standards for the world to witness had not entered the equation. I felt that whatever my brother did would not be good enough for his parents, but for me as long as he felt happy in his chosen way, and avoided being caught breaking the law, fine to break it as long as you don't get caught, all was good. He used whatever skills it takes to work in factory stores and the best job he had as a stores man was at Coventry Climax where engines for high performance cars were built, not that this impressed our father.

To repeat, how Syd managed his life was his business and yet, reluctant as I am to criticise him, aspects of his life were, and remain, puzzling to me as someone who has striven, often against 'Man's bedevilment and God's', to follow a path as personally comfortable and unconstrained as possible. I enjoyed our talks and our complimentary style of wit and humour, if one found something funny the other could always share it, and the man read, actual books which we could discuss. The models he made were also superb. One further thing in Syd's favour, he was for many years, a blood donor and once told me you take it out and I put it in, this with a deprecating smile. Well said brother, well done...

I enjoyed the times I spent at my brother's house playing with the kids who were, strangely, not allowed out on a Sunday, puzzling as this restriction had nothing to do with religion as far as I could tell and I could never understand what significance Sunday had other than a religious one although I've been told the kids attended Sunday school I have no recollection of that on the Sundays I stayed with the family, perhaps they were given time off for what was perceived as good behaviour during my visits. I would usually forget that they were obliged to stay indoors and out into the garden we'd go when nothing would be said to me about it. The boys were not exactly well-behaved and could be very destructive, I say they but it could be that only one of them was the culprit. When Syd who previously had an allotment fenced off the bottom of the garden to grow vegetables in no time at all the fence was wrecked, the little gate off its hinges and the project abandoned. A rockery went the same way, planted up with perennials when first I saw it but the next time being used to ride bikes over, the plants trampled and flattened and the greenhouse cum shed he'd made from found materials and a covering of plastic sheet first full of holes that had been poked through and at the last wrecked totally with the remains of the sheeting reduced to loose tatters.

The boys were mostly friendly toward me and no real trouble and I was flattered to hear a confrontation with each arguing that I was *his* uncle. I hope I didn't favour one above the other but it is possible and if it was so did they notice? Did they also respect their father? This too is possible but if true it was hard to tell, if he took steps to curb their depredations they were ineffective. I heard him fiercely threaten them on occasion but they just seemed to think it funny.

I know all his children missed him after his early death as I, and I'm sure they, still do. The older boys being young at the time of their vandalism may have forgotten about it but if they remember I hope they recall also their father's tolerance.

They were more afraid of their mother's actions; when cross she would take off her slipper and throw it at them, why bother to stir any further, but she couldn't see them ruining Syd's efforts from her chair in front of the fire and television and may not have been too bothered anyway. If this reads as unfair, I admit the truth, it possibly is to an extent! Vi was invariably kind to me in my childhood as already mentioned and could be energetic when required and organising the latest party would be one of those times. There were a great many parties in that house and having left behind the select company of Ivy Walkites, who wouldn't be inclined to celebrate to excess. The flow of partying however provoked the obviously contemptuous comment from Dad any excuse for a party.

When at their house minus my parents it was often fun, particularly the parties and talking with Syd or playing with the kids. I have a vivid memory of knocking a balloon back and forth trying to keep it in the air with Vi joining in as well, a happy time though Syd was busy in the kitchen and took no part.

Once two younger boys came along I stopped buying Christmas and birthday presents for all as five stretched my resources too far and one couldn't have favourites. Also contributing to my decision was the realisation that my efforts were not really appreciated as shown by a present I'd saved my pocket money to buy for my niece and Mum and me wrapped being wrongly attributed to Vi's brother. I was astonished to hear it asserted that he had bought it for her and when I protested to find I was contradicted. So no more presents, and about a year later when Leslie asked what I'd bought him for his birthday Vi jumped in and said he 'Ought to know that uncle Derek never buys him anything'!

Chapter 27

Not everyone has a memory as detailed as mine and to be charitable the fact that my contributions on the gift front may just have been forgotten. I have forgotten much too and apologise here for leaving out of these pages anyone who feels I might have included them. Some will have had a mention in my previous two books and others may yet find themselves recalled later.

As a child the continuing presence of well known, some well-loved, neighbours was important to me also long term friendships, but making friends among patients and staff during one hospital admission and finding them gone the next emphasised the temporary nature of alliances and companionship. It could be that my mostly unconscious need to separate hospital and home to the extent of rejecting the continued friendship offered once home grew from this cause. Perhaps also the often repeated prediction of my early death sharpened the need for consistency most children feel, to a craving for continuity ensuring I seek whatever evidence might be available. All these years later I still wonder what came next in the lives of those I knew, some for only a very few weeks, and have latterly come to understand that they would have forgotten me years since and that my remembering them has been a rejection of death, theirs and my own. To be remembered by someone is to be alive for that person, are the three books chronicling my life only a last desperate effort to thwart death?

I could list the neighbours tediously detailing each, but apart from one, or perhaps two, enemies I respected and in some cases liked them all so will select only a few to elaborate on.

Annie Barkis and her daughter Louise lived a little further up the street and sporadically Louise and I would spend time together and were friends. I was easily exasperated, not always good to be around and Louise had female friends she sensibly preferred. I vividly recall the time she came to me complaining that some other little girl had 'Taken June off her.' this I already knew as I'd seen the two new friends walking arm in arm ignoring Louise. Did I, she asked want to play in her garden? as this usually consisted of mud pies which seemed a useless occupation, and as I knew she would chunter on about the perfidious June I snarled no I didn't and stumped off in disgust.

Not very friendly, but I wasn't invariably prickly and for some time I spent many happy hours playing at her home until it was reported to me by Mum that Mr Barkis, had complained I was there too often, this hurt and it got my alternative to the angry reaction, avoidance. I never went there again.

Further evidence of my touchy and downright cheeky approach to the world and its frustrations emerged when Louise's grandmother upset me and my usual unrestrained response followed. I had a bag of sweets and walked down the entry past Louise's garden with a very obviously full mouth, bag of sweets in hand. I saw this lady in the garden as I turned the corner and decided to play the little gentleman by offering her the bag and asking would she like one and the closer I got the more satisfactory the idea became; a chance to rehearse another new strategy to add to opening doors and walking on the outside when accompanying females young and old. I liked to try and inhabit the skin of those I'd read about and fancied the role of Gawain 'Who never would uncurtis be to any lady' and anyway a reputation for courtesy might get you anywhere. If you criticise this as much too knowing and cynical in a nine-year-old, congratulations it was! Alas, more good intentions turned to dross, as I reached her she asked, with an irritating adult instructing the young smile 'aren't you going to offer me one?' Thwarted and furious, after momentarily setting my teeth at her I responded with 'No you bugger, you're not having one for asking' and briskly strode on. Many years later I smiled on listening to a performance of Under Milk Wood at the line 'I want to be good boyo, but no one'll let me.' the context undoubtedly different but something I felt at nine years.

Louise's grandmother never forgot the incident and neither did I; it probably taught her a very valuable lesson!

A year or so after this Louise and her mother Annie came round to see us and imbibe the cup of tea that was habitual fare when neighbours met to chat, Annie made the interesting remark that she could tell if only one grain of sugar adulterated her tea, this information was unbelievable and I stored it for later. Louise was bored it being toward the end of the school holidays and both mothers thought it would be a good idea for Louise and me to have a knitting competition and as I never turned down an opportunity to win I agreed; a leg brace was not going to affect the outcome and knitting so gentle as to be completely non-haemorhagenic. After I'd been shown the rudiments of knitting it was agreed that whoever had knitted the longest scarf after two days would be declared the winner. I worked carefully and neatly in one colour, with no dropped stitches, every row the same length and two days later I had to show for it a six by ten inch something, so heavy and solid that if ever it had reached scarf length would have dragged a wearer to the ground or dislocated he neck; I'd not been told about tension. Louise's version was made up of scraps of wool, ludicrously multi coloured, thin, full of holes, and showers of dropped stitches with some sections only an inch wide and others six or seven and to my chagrin she was declared the winner as her effort was over two feet long and although I protested the state of it the contest was about length. Now it was my turn for a valuable lesson.

Three lessons, always be sure of the rules when taking part in a competition, female solidarity and ruthlessness take precedence over common sense and that I had no skill at knitting and no inclination to have more to do with it finding it tedious and fiddly anyway. Given my irritation it's a wonder that I didn't tell them where to store the needles. I decided instead that the time had come to test Annie Barkis' famed sugar detection facility.

Into the next cup of tea I smuggled a single grain of sugar, no reaction whatsoever, I repeated the experiment again with the same result and thereafter doubled the amount each time until the equivalent of almost an eighth of a flat teaspoon provoked the response of a slight frown and a glance at the cup. Having proved her assertion wrong and checked the actual level of tolerance the experiment was over.

The immediate neighbours, the Morells one side the Turleys the other certainly gave me the sense of continuity I needed at least during my younger years, though before I left home both families had been replaced as the families sold up. As a young child I thought things would remain the same if not forever then as far into the future as I was prepared to see. It didn't take long before this illusion was demolished by deaths and adverse circumstance but although everything had changed before I left home I felt shocked when my parents sold up and moved to Cornwall.

The Turleys had been the first to leave the trio of adjoining homes, I'd known the parents as Aunt and Uncle and my oldest friend Martin I felt I'd known since birth. Our friendship resumed on my return from Corley Open air School, some friendships did not, and on meeting again he showed me a foam rubber Donald Duck toy that with fingers placed inside could be manipulated to contort the face and simulate talk. He pointed it toward me and uttered 'Aww phooey', at which I politely smiled although not understanding what he was getting at. I didn't recognise this as a catch phrase, three years sequestered at a residential school had left me ignorant of the culture of childhood as it had developed. This episode while not particularly exciting or funny is an indication of the difficulty I felt once home. I was embarrassed when I couldn't make out why he said those strange words to me and worked out an erroneous scenario. The face poised on his fingers was a well known character that was preoccupied, like the Dandy's Plum McDuff, with eating and phooey was his way of saying food.

Despite the regular misunderstandings we remained friends right up until the unfortunate day when everything changed on his mother suddenly disappearing with another man.

It came as a shock both to Martin and the man I'd always known as Uncle and he went to live with his Gran, the dog in both our lives, Rover, was no more and the house was sold.

The fact is that I had seen more of Rover than Martin once back from Corley as I went on to home tuition while he went on to the local secondary school.

A remarkable dog, Rover, he could not be prevented from slipping his collar, straining back against the tether holding him close to his kennel during school hours as it was impossible to keep him from finding his way out of the garden without it. Once his Houdini act had been achieved he'd be off on his travels unless I could persuade him to stay with me. He roamed over a wide area and it was possible to hear kids shouting 'Here Rover' around all the surrounding streets, and a couple of miles away I would see him chasing a thrown ball or running around with other dogs on many a green space.

When in my company he would eventually get bored and want to be on his travels once he realised we weren't going to go for a country walk. I knew the signs but being so clever he could elude me easily by sniffing along a fence or wall moving a little further away with each sniff.

Chapter 28

If I noticed before he was completely beyond reach he'd come back when told but once I was sufficiently distracted by whatever game I was playing he'd consider it the correct distance to be safe and ignore my shouts to come back, trotting purposefully on, the only indication that he heard, the laying back of his ears.

Coming in his gate after one of our walks we both saw two rats eating from his food bowl, he gave a cross between a whine and a growl, a curious noise, and raced down the path toward them, but they outmanoeuvred him and fled back up the path in my direction with him following. I stepped aside and when the rats got towards the gate they split up one right, one left and in the moment it took him to decide which to follow they had gone. Any hole in the ground big enough to accommodate a rat was vigorously excavated sometimes receiving attention for an hour or so.

Birds were also troublesome to him flying down and snatching hair from his back for nesting material but rats were his enemies and on one occasion he saved me from a two-legged variety that came over to me when sitting with Rover on a doorstep down at the shops. The strangely disturbing man approached and with hello sonny is that your dog reached forward presumably to stroke. As he bent Rover suddenly jumped clear over him and startled he turned and walked swiftly on. His interest may have been quite innocent but he unnerved us both.

Mr and Mrs Morell our next door neighbours on the other side both died during my childhood but their son and daughter remained until she married and moved out. The son married and his wife moved in. I missed seeing Ann but Edgar remaining gave the continuity I needed. The family were invariably good to me, the new spouses too.

When the Morells left, a strange couple moved in and my parents and they had a kitchen extension built as a combined job. I don't suppose the husband was that strange but his wife's fixed smile was not the least of her strangeness.

The collaboration on the kitchens was somewhat fraught, one problem being the insistence by the other party on taking up the lowest quote much against Dad's better judgement. Sure enough the build did not run smoothly, the building inspectors not accepting work that had been done and time and money wasted on rectification. Then Dad insisted that bricks stored in our garden had gone missing, the police were involved and Dad, possibly, accused the builders. I say possibly because they came knocking on the door demanding to see my father as the police had interviewed them. I was there on my own and they went away. The outcome I never knew except that other builders took over. The original crew had not been a genuine firm, arriving with their tools on a handcart, but I was never convinced they took the bricks, they gave the impression of being puzzled and hurt more than outraged on confronting me. Whether the allegation was fair or not Dad got his way in the end and a firm of local bona fide builders completed the job.

Our new neighbour fished for pike and in friendship gave my parents two specimens he'd caught, these were discretely disposed of as Dad said they were disgusting things that nibbled canal suicides, dead cats and filthy rubbish. Dad being Dad and pike being predators I doubted his logic, after all he said the same thing about mackerel and they obviously caught smaller fish for a living.

The man's wife was an extremely peculiar person with one of those faces that even at rest harbour an involuntary smile around the mouth as the corners are permanently turned up. Never having visited their home I cannot say if it was spick and span beyond all reason but the garden exhibited every sign of a mind obsessed with tidiness.

The craziness was confirmed when on almost reaching our door after coming in the back way I was startled as a shower of stones came flying from her garden, thrown so hard they crashed into the fence on the Smith's side. I'd just left Al and some of the stones passed over into his garden and the crash as the rest hit had him sticking his head over and asking me what I was doing. I pointed out where they'd come from and the woman's voice came floating over telling me to stop throwing stones in her garden. This was not one of my admittedly nefarious deeds and I reported it to my parents who asked other neighbours if they knew what was going on.

Mr Osbourne who lived next door to this woman on the other side told Mum 'It's your turn now is it', as he'd had the same accusation hurled at him. It turned out that the woman picked every stone, minute twig or piece of brick off the exposed earth in her garden every day, then raked it over to leave a level surface of pristine brown earth only to find next day more stones and other debris. Anyone with any sense, and most with an interest in gardening and reality have that, should know that freshly tilled earth may look stone free but after even the lightest of showers washes off the soil the concealed stones become revealed. As the wearisome stones appeared in the beds and borders but not on the immaculately trimmed lawn only someone with hours to spend and superhuman hand and eye coordination could have perpetuated the imaginary outrage and would surely have been caught.

Strolling home up the same path some months later I noticed that the kitchen curtains next door were alight and flapping outside the open window. I admit I hesitated for a few moments sure that if I called out I'd be accused of somehow setting fire to the curtains and the thought serve her right if I let them burn also assailed me, I recalled however that our kitchen was at risk and called the woman, it took several yells of fire and her name before I heard a yelp and water extinguished the blaze. I waited to be accused or thanked but neither of these things happened.

After only a couple of years they moved away and a middle-aged couple and son moved in. I remember very little about them except the son's twenty-first birthday celebration in a pub or club and us accepting the invitation to attend. The son quite obviously resented my presence and assumed a long face whenever our eyes met, perhaps I had forgotten to congratulate him, or never having met me he had formed an adverse opinion in lieu. I do know no one bothered to introduce us. The only other memory of the party is of Dad telling me he didn't realise I could drink so much beer and maintain sobriety and this I took to be complimentary in some way. An amount of mutual distrust had grown between us, never spoken and not dislike exactly, not on my part at least but a kind of wariness from a lack of understanding and disappointment.

Obviously I disappointed the man as much as he disappointed me. I know my chronic illness caused him embarrassment at times, but my lack of interest in things mechanical must have made it as difficult for him to understand me as I found it difficult to understand him. Quite suddenly when I was about twelve years old, apropos nothing, he informed me that he intended to bring a Mike home, and I suspected this to be another of the employees who were occasionally invited to lunch but no; the mike was a micrometer and with a look of anticipation he informed me that he would show me how to use it. I had no enthusiasm for the lesson, I doubted that I would ever have need of the knowledge, mechanics and engineering held no fascination and my education in maths or even simple arithmetic continuing to be neglected at 'special' school I was apprehensive that I might appear a fool. The threatened mike never appeared so it seems my lack of interest, sadly for him, killed the idea. I have reason to believe that both parents were unaware of my situation at school, partly my fault as I never explained how awful I found the place not expecting anything to be achieved by speaking out. Here's how little Dad understood of me, my friends and the administrative workings of the school.

Chapter 29

I arrived home to be told: Your Dad's very annoyed; he's had a letter from your teacher! Later when Dad returned and after he'd perused the headlines in the local paper he took from a drawer the annoying letter and confronted me with his version of the contents 'I've had a letter from your teacher, I'm told you're not being a good scholar'. Puzzled by this, after all scholarship didn't exist at the school, I said nothing and he handed me the letter to read for myself. Needless to say it did not come from my 'teacher' but a visiting school doctor who had taken an interest in me since my earliest hospital admissions. Why not the school head? Perhaps the news of my contumacy was thought better communicated by a friend. The letter spoke of disappointment advising that 'Derek refuses to take part in the life of the school'. No explanation of exactly what I refused, no wonder Dad had difficulty understanding! He told me I must do my best and that, as far as I know, was the end of the matter.

I worked out that the 'life of the school' that I eschewed was the instruction to join the choir and the singing group and the total lack of interest in the house points system; I had no interest in the competition not caring which house won the shield or cup and the only house points I had to offer at the end of the week were the three or four I awarded myself as recompense for attendance.

Dad was a fascinating study, well worth observing. The fencing on Al's side of the garden he claimed was Al's parent's responsibility and when the fence the other side needed attention that was the responsibility of whomever the neighbours were at the time. It may well be that he believed his own mistaken explanations of the position but I incline to the idea that saving money influenced his thinking and his memory.

I well remember his telling me 'You cost me five bob a month when you were at Corley', was this complaint or recognition of what a bargain he'd had, five shillings a month to maintain life in his offspring? He might have been lamenting the fact that my pocket money, a shilling a week, was only a little less per week than he'd been required to pay before and now he had to feed and clothe me too!

My father was by no means one dimensional but a complex of often conflicting points of view, mildly racist as a great many were back then not having had the benefit of contact with those of a different ethnicity, he nevertheless regretted the decision of Jewish neighbours to emigrate to Israel, admired the teacher who refused to make her class salute the flag on Empire Day and felt contempt for his business partner who laughingly bragged about hitting people with six foot long sticks called lathis with the army in India. Generous and tight-fisted, steady and inconsistent, knowledgeable and ignorant he kept my interest as it was impossible to predict what he would do or say next. Add to this mixture his disabling self-consciousness and his ability, if approached in a gentle way, to acknowledge his foolishness with a sheepish smile and it becomes obvious why from a small child I found him puzzling.

He could be fun at times and I was always sure he loved me, but when very young I couldn't understand why he never came to see me in hospital. Later I saw that he found it too painful to visit the children's ward where two of his infant offspring had died. Once my admissions to hospital saw me placed in a side ward attached to a men's medical ward he visited me at least once a week, usually Sunday.

For the next few years whenever a spell on Cleaver, Gulson Road Hospital, came along he and Mum visited me together and this continued after I left the care of Mr. Parry-Williams on the two occasions I was admitted to Coventry and Warwick in my late teens.

The last time I was admitted to a Coventry hospital, until returning to Coventry in the seventies, was notable for a couple of characters among my fellow patients, my own mad exploits and Dad revealing either a lack of knowledge or an intriguing straight faced comedic portrayal of an ignoramus.

Mr Jones, a farmer, was hoping to have his hip problem sorted and told me about his grandson, a three year old who had been seen to clamber on and off his toy tractor in a stiff manner with many groans and oohs. When asked if he was alright he responded by explaining he wanted to do it as his grandad did! By now I had given up on my ambition to farm so didn't ask for a job.

The other patient worked as a barman at the flying club and this young man, probably only a couple of years older than me was filthy. At least his feet were, and his mind too. I saw his feet when he jumped out of bed and came across to loan me a book which he said was good and that I would like. His feet and lower calves were black with filth and the book with a lurid cover and the fetching title Sorority Sluts had no plot and was just an excuse for a catalogue of sometimes disgusting sex, in short a book as dirty as his feet.

I suppose this character was handsome as at least one of the nurses didn't mind his unwashed feet, stunted vocabulary and loutish manners as she allowed herself to be briefly man-handled around the room, danced with I suppose, and leered at thereafter each time she entered.

I often drank beer at folk clubs but also imbibed with selected friends another alcoholic beverage and why should hospital hold me back? So I asked Al to bring me in my favourite tipple and despite some reservations he complied.

My parents supplied the lime juice cordial so after supper I resorted to a couple of crafty vodka and lime being careful not to let my companions catch sight, after all sharing was out of the question. The inconspicuous number four in the four-bedder would not have been a problem, the farmer would have refused to break the rules and blackfoot would have ruined my game by insisting on drinking too much.

I had my parents bring in my tape recorder and the tape on which I had recorded various noises that appealed to me, a passing train, a toilet flushing, a neighbour shouting at me 'You've started again have yer, you bugger you!' and various clicks, doors being knocked and others. This tape I would play quietly with the recorder hidden in the locker. It was possible to hear but not to understand. The consensus of opinion among my victims, the nurses, was that it was pigeons on the roof.

My parents visited and Dad showed an unusual amount of interest in the sky, going to the window and gazing up for seconds at a time before returning to the bedside with a pensive look when I asked what interested him Mum jumped in saying 'He's worried'. Thus prompted he explained that shortly a hard moon landing was going to take place and bits of the moon might fall on us. To say I was astonished doesn't convey just how jaw dropping this statement was. That a technically minded person such as I'd always thought him could give credence to a delusional idea stunned me. I said nothing. The moon mission was one of the Ranger moon shots most likely 9 on the 21st. March 1965 which fits with my age at the time. This was not the first hard moon landing the USSR having accomplished it some years before so why this should have generated fear is a mystery; now unburdened he told me of his other fear.

'And I wish they'd drop this stupid idea of a channel tunnel'. Oh no, I thought, he's now going to lay the silly bugger notion of an invasion on me but no, it was worse. When I protested that it appeared to be danger free he glared eyes bulging and slammed his fist into the palm of his hand and snarling 'Don't you know what would happen if that thing collapsed in the middle? The whole of England would be flooded!' Back to window went Dad and I tried to convince myself that he was joking. This was a forlorn hope as both parents continued to look worried and he tutted with his usual jerk of the head and asked if we didn't have enough problems without adding to them.

Here was my father, an ace mechanic and capable metal worker showing incredible ignorance of physics, he had a questioning mind and would often wonder aloud about various phenomena but when I'd offer an explanation he would ignore it and repeat his query. I had believed that he chose to dismiss my explanation as wrong or couldn't accept that I knew more about the subject than him; after his regrettable opinions revealed on that day I could see that he hadn't understood my explanations as I'd credited him with more knowledge than he'd possessed. Without a firm foundation new information often sounds unlikely. At the time I also blamed a relative Dad liked to visit whose opinions were equally rum.

Chapter 30

The pair of them contributed an infinitely amusing and satisfying incident for me to enjoy when they fitted a new letter box with integral knocker to this cousin's front door. I came along as they decided that the hole in the door had been perfectly adjusted to provide the snuggest of fits. Just one problem I interjected only to be told 'Who's doing the job?' and ordered to mind my own business. I took the advice watching and waiting until they bolted the contraption to the door and were standing back to admire their efforts, 'Ah We've made a good job of that'. I stepped forward agreeing with them but pointing out the one problem. 'It fits perfectly but it's upside down' and lifted the knocker upwards to knock the door. They asked why I didn't warn them, I responded that I had been content to mind my own business, smiled and went in to see the daughter of the house.

Early in January 2002 I received a letter from a woman telling me that a family member of hers, a seventeen year old girl, had a relationship during 1968/69 with a man named Derek Haughton who frequented the Baginton Oak pub, the relationship ending late in 1968 with no further contact. The inference impossible to miss was that the girl became pregnant. I wrote straight back to assure the woman that I was not the father of the child not having even known a Janet at the time nor ever having been in the Baginton Oak back then. I did wonder however, just how brief the 'relationship' had been and if the fact that the Baginton Oak and the Flying Club bar being so close pointed to blackfoot and if he might have used my name; paranoia, coincidence or evidence for another Derek Haughton living in Coventry?

The week or so spent with the farmer, the grotesquery and another in the four -bedder saw the end of my association with Coventry and Warwickshire hospital but not with strange cases of mistaken identity, confusion around my name and just plain mystery.

Why was I told there was a person waiting at reception to give me my lift home as arranged when I'd driven to the maternity hospital when my son was born? Wondering what the hell, I rushed down to reception to find no one waiting and the receptionist telling me that they had left. On keeping an appointment at the nearby hospital concerning how to cope with pain I was told that the new consultant was pleased to see that I had been up to the ward to collect the relaxation tapes left for me by her predecessor and produced a letter from the ward sister saying that I had collected them. Two problems with the statement: tapes had never been mentioned to me and I had never been up to the ward, in short the matter was news to me. Some months later I received a letter asking if I would like to switch my pension plan as an employee of the NHS. This came as a surprise as I'd never worked for and wasn't employed by, the NHS.

Several times I was accosted by people asking where I'd been and who didn't believe me when I told them they had the wrong person. One chap telling me to come off it and plaintively asking why was I being like that? As he walked away he looked back with a frown. A shop keeper on my entrance was convinced he knew me and asked why I hadn't been in his shop for some months, had I been ill? I'd never been in the shop before but by this time I was so used to being mistaken for my double that I told him no, I had been working away. Cars would beep at me, the occupants waving and smiling or folks shout across the street to ask how I was doing, none of these people I recognised.

I received a card from the library telling me the book I had ordered was ready for me to collect; I hadn't ordered a book and had no particular interest in the contents of this one The Diseases of Tropical Salt Water Fish. I took the card in and a staff member pointed out that the address and name of the book were always filled in by the person making the request. Catholic as my reading is I definitely had not requested the book, leaving the librarian and me equally puzzled

Some years later I was threatened by a debt collection firm for the repayment of a loan I'd never had, this was quickly sorted out but perhaps taken together some of these things show that there is/was another Derek Haughton in Coventry, whether a double in looks exists is also a strong possibility, but the two together?

One person often mentioned in all three of the books that make up my autobiographical trilogy is Alan S, Al, my next door neighbour, friend and co-conspirator. As boys we built bombs and a deadly cannon which fired either a fistful of lead pellets or a ball bearing with a black-powder propellant, experimented horticulturally, conspired against an enemy or two and shared fun and laughter whenever together.

Picked up by bus each morning and taken off to special school we would go our separate ways as he was in a lower class being a couple of years younger and meet up again on the journey home. Consequently the pattern of my behaviour that had developed separating home from hospital continued at special school where I managed, not consciously I add, to leave school friendships at school. Old home alliances had disappeared as others went on to local secondary schools so it was a happy situation when Al's friends visited him at home and these became my friends too.

When Al left school he acquired a job in an office, a few of the old gang were still around and John from Al's office joined the crew. Several of us liked folk music and that proportion of the friends started going to folk clubs together. Gradually the rest dropped away until me, Al, John and Dave were the only ones left. Dave had been in Al's class at school but had moved back to his home city of Birmingham from where he brought friends to one of the clubs and we would go over to Birmingham to various parties and gatherings. After one of these it was suggested we move on to a club at Yardley so our ill-assorted tribe headed off, but of course being in the middle of the day it looked obviously closed. Al and I stayed one side of the road while the others went across to bang on the door and try to enforce entry. One using a wheelchair two others crutches and Al said, dragging on an imaginary cigarette, both of us had this character in our respective cache of impersonations, 'Cor blimey, it's like a bleedin' cripples convention.'

A few times some of us went to a night club, the Night Owl, in Leicester but it really wasn't my kind of thing; live bands the only good point, the music too loud, the lighting subdued almost to darkness, very few places to sit and in the words of a song of recent years: I think it's really quite obscene, what kind of people go to meet people in a place you can't be heard or seen. Kicked out at 5-30am what was there to do but wait for the bus service to start up. The first time we went on to Nottingham to check the theory that the best looking women in the country were to be found there.

There *was* pulchritude in plenty but no more or less than elsewhere so we broadened our search. During his holidays from work we went 'walkabout' quotes because we would get on local buses rather than walk, on one expedition reaching Stratford-on-Avon where we switched from Midland Red to Stratford Blue buses to Cheltenham. Spending a couple of nights in bed and breakfast establishments on the way and failing to find anywhere to sleep one night spent it out in the cold, partly on a park bench and the rest of the time walking about to keep warm. Apart from ogling a string of sixth formers being escorted two by two from a famous

Cheltenham school to who knows where, having a young boy offer to scrump apples for us when we were miles from anywhere, which he did, over a fence and out again and earning the scorn of a car full of youths as we crossed the road at a t-junction thinking we had plenty of time, I remember very little. The last two incidents came after the park bench night when we took a dose of one of the wake you up pills readily available to the young but usually reserved by us for all night parties in Birmingham, at one of which I found myself refusing the daintiest morsel on the menu, Stephanie.

Steph, Steph how could I behave so well in resisting and me, as we used to say, as randy as a cartload of monkeys? We'd met when Dave Martin had brought several of his friends from Birmingham to meet me, a procedure he was wont to indulge in, showing me off like an agent trying to impress an entrepreneur. We were talking or I was talking and they were hanging on my every word with Dave saying 'See, see what I mean?' at my slightest witticism when a record was played on the radio which had the line 'Twiddling my thumbs.' and I suited my actions to the words. Steph was the only one who noticed! I liked her immediately. Pretty and slight, she intrigued me.

At the party she made it plain that I could have her there and then but I had heard that her father had died only a couple of weeks before and she was barely of age if that.

Chapter 31

I felt that she was seeking not exactly a replacement but something more than any of us there could offer so for those reasons and not wanting to be lying on the landing in full view as one or two couples were I regretfully chose to be impervious.

Shortly after this Al went on his own to a club in London frequented by patrons from many different ethnic backgrounds, and a bunch of these started asking each other's origins. Al having a very freckled face and blue lips owing to his heart condition intrigued them and was soon asked where he came from. He was delighted to tell me this story, but not so delighted about what happened as he left the club. He was stopped and searched and found to have about his person more of the pills mentioned earlier. Now he would have to go back and appear before the magistrates and wanted me to go with him.

A story was concocted which I felt sure would see him O K. Here's how it went: someone offered to sell him the pills in the club, he bought them because he did not want to be laughed at as timid. He succumbed for that reason only and wouldn't have taken them owing to his heart condition, with the medical evidence this did the trick. No fine, the magistrate said having to come back there was punishment enough and that he hoped he'd learned his lesson! Success and joy for us both and that evening and night we spent around Soho. Talking Kierkegaard and Nietzsche, of whom and their works we knew very little, only what we had learned from hanging around a café in the Bull Ring Centre in Birmingham until our encounter, at three in the morning, with a beatnik, forerunner of the hippy, who walked with a silver topped cane in one hand and a beatnik girl on his other arm. The teach-in and advice filled an hour and we wished each other good fortune and departed. Earlier we noted with a nod and a smile, the strippers who hurried from club to club with a small case containing the tricks of the trade, one of whom even smiled back. Two thoughts stirred; it would be intimidating to be recognised by erstwhile punters, not that we were, and how strange it was to know that the quite modestly dressed young women would soon be available to view naked by those willing to pay. I reminded Al of the time a couple of years before when we and several other members of the gang had passed a club and a doorman jingling a pocket full of cash had told us 'Come in lads, no posing.' a reference to the relaxing of the rule requiring posed nude tableaux only, and how I had failed to elicit a laugh with a reference to Oscar Wilde by saying 'How did he know'. Al got it but perhaps fortunately the others didn't.

It got chilly as the hours crawled on towards dawn and we followed out beatnik's guide to warm ourselves with coffee in the café reserved for Covent Garden workers until challenged by some hulking brute as not working in the market and kicked out to spend the rest of the night rejecting the advances of those touting for various kinds of custom until morning and Euston coach station.

Reading about my travels might lead you to think that bleeds had become few and far between, this was not the case. The minor, probably boring exploits came between episodes of bleeding and the hard work needed to recover. Then Al bought a second hand bubble car, an Isetta, and Dad taught him to drive. He and I spent many happy hours driving round in the bubble. Of an evening we'd often go for a drive around the local lanes sometimes stopping at a pub The Jolly Colliers for a drink, this being on the outskirts of the city, and then on into the countryside.

The folk club Al, me, John and Dave patronized with our other friends from Birmingham decided to ask the members what acts they would like to see and sent round paper to each table at 'half-time'. Our answers were I'm afraid totally facetious, the singing postman, the singing nuns, the singing track workers and Dave's topping off, the singing spastics. When gathered up one of the lists caused consternation and the organisers and resident singers looked shocked and could be seen speculating on which table had perpetrated the sick joke. They looked at us but shook their heads, surely not us who had obviously disabled members in the crew. I wasn't entirely comfortable with Dave's contribution, cerebral palsy people were the closest to heroes for me, carrying on with their lives in spite of being stared at and treated as though mentally ill or slow witted often by people below my contempt, ablebods whose ability to think had been squashed by standard education if they'd ever been equipped to think at all. For such chronically sick and/or disabled people were covered by the term spastics so in that sense Dave was laughing at all of us.

Dave's family originally from Birmingham had moved back to Stechford once he'd left special school and kept a shop in which he worked, driving a red reliant van refueling as sparingly as possible. On one forecourt paying the pump attendant, remember those? With the words 'Here you are my man, two coins of the realm and don't forget its treble stamps!' The remains of the gang spent hours in that van travelling to holidays and adventures.

That Easter we made up a convoy, Steve on his newly purchased motorbike followed by the Isetta bubble car and Dave's Reliant van. At Malvern Wells we found an unofficial camping place up a steep track that leveled out into a flat area big enough to take all three vehicles and the tent we'd been loaned. Al drove the bubble up on his own, a slightly dangerous procedure and in my mind's eye I can see him now bouncing about on the rough track. We pitched the tent and I for one was appalled to find it had no ground sheet and was not a tent but the fly sheet from a tent but too late now to do anything about the omissions. I took a walk further up the hill and took out my mouth organ and started playing, improvising around a short sequence of notes.

It sounded astonishingly good as though, to slip into mysticism, I had a guide. Then I walked up further and stood overlooking the ancient sight known as British Camp. Further mysticism, I felt sure that beside me also looking down was a man with a spear and a rough fur cape turned against the prevailing wind. The spear butt rested on the ground and his leg curved round it for extra stability. Smiling he pointed to the earthworks and I felt him in my mind call me brother and friend. These intimations and the moving shadows of clouds over the landscape below me, I call the Malvern levitation. Certainly a strange state of mind had overcome me and I had run with it. When I came back down my friends were looking puzzled and Steve often one to challenge me said 'I thought you said you couldn't play.' that's when I knew that I'd not been mistaken about the quality of the music at least.

The night proved cold in that draughty apology for a tent and the situation deteriorated further when I awoke to the sounds of furtive movements outside followed by a smothered cough or two and I gently roused the others. A whispered plan was hatched and on my shout we all stuck our heads out. Absolute panic ensued as a number of sheep that had been attracted by the new phenomenon of the tent scattered, knocking into guy ropes and yanking out tent pegs. Sleeping under a half collapsed fly sheet was an unpleasant experience but on the other hand I now understood that a sheep cough sounds human, fair enough as a great many humans behave like sheep.

Al and I gained much satisfaction in mockery, getting onto buses and making comments on the weather etc.

to older passengers in broad accents just as they would, 'Ah, lovely weather for ducks'. 'A bit parky today en it?' We got an undeserved reputation as good lads. Though strangely, we had an enemy among the old codgers, always muttering and looking at us with a scowl even when we kept our mouths shut. One night after an evening in the city centre we went upstairs at the terminus to wait for the bus to leave and opened the little sliding window to shout goodnight to another friend who was making for a different bus. 'Good night, Tom' our enemy jumped up out of his seat crying you filthy mouthed little devils, I'll get the inspector to put you off! He rushed down the stairs and out into the bus station, where's an inspector when you need one? The driver arrived and the bus took off leaving the maniac behind.

Al and Dave had both been born with heart defects and when they reached adulthood both were tested to see if, now there growing phase was complete, the defects could be corrected by surgery. The last time I saw Dave was when we attended a folk concert in Birmingham refusing to stand for the national anthem at the end of the evening. When he crossed the road to catch the bus home he had to rest to catch his breath and I knew the procedure on his heart was inevitable. Shortly after I moved into the high rise building with my first wife he sent me a letter as he was about to go into hospital and included in it the words to the song The Parting Glass. He must have realised the danger that he would not survive and indeed he never came out of the anaesthetic, I'd been warned by the enclosure, quote: Since it falls unto my lot to rise and go while you do not,

I'll gently rise and softly call goodnight and joy be with you all, but was saddened to think of his no longer being in the world.

The results from the tests that both my friends had gone through had revealed that Dave might benefit from surgery but that it should be left as long as possible having no guarantee and that for Al there was no chance of him surviving the procedure. Instead his condition was monitored, medication prescribed and a pint of blood removed every few weeks. Knowing his interest in gardening it was suggested he take the bag full of blood home and use it as a nitrogenous fertiliser.

Chapter 32

The suggestion was politely declined and we laughed together as he recounted his reasoning, there is after all something romantically macabre about a gardener spilling his life blood to encourage the roses and what if he tripped over on the bus home the bag bursting to a spreading pool panicking some and nauseating others?

An incident guaranteed to raise a smile when recalled is the bus stop fist fight. We were waiting for the bus home in the early evening when a burly drunken navvy type asked the way to the gents, we directed him around the corner but although setting out in the right direction he instead staggered up a flight of steps into a building where a dance class was taking place. Expecting an irate accusation of misleading him we were hoping the bus would come when he shot out of the door and down the steps miraculously keeping his feet and of all things eating an apple. He strolled towards us not obviously aggressive when another similar person turned up and asked 'Is he bothering you lads.' and before we could answer a growling argument broke out. An Irishman and a Scotsman we learnt as each told the other to get back to their own country. Then two things happened, a roaring fight and the arrival of the bus. We jumped aboard, the bus drove off and we watched the brawlers fade into the distance.

Some years later, during one of my long haired stints yet another drunk left the wall he was sitting on and aggressively approached saying right in my face 'What's going on Jesus?' my safety depended on the best reply and the words came out as I thought them 'How in Christ's name should I know?' he reeled back as though hit or pushed in the chest for two or three yards and thwacked down on his backside. I went on my way rejoicing.

I assume that in Dave's case the procedure was a desperate last attempt to save his life but that Al could not have been helped at all. Al survived for a few more good years but also died at only twenty- eight.

Both Al and my father died when I, Estelle, my second wife and children lived off Far Gosford Street and both deaths came as an unexpected blow. Dad had visited Coventry and surprised me by going along to his old school, at that time known as Eastfields but in his boyhood East Street. This was startling, it should have told me something, it was so out of character. He told us he'd been very impressed by the fact that all the children of various racial backgrounds got on so well together to which I replied that no one had yet fouled up their minds with irrelevant bull, to which he merely nodded. He seemed very pensive. I had the impression that he wanted to say more, that something was on his mind but whatever it was he kept it to himself. That was the last time I saw him as shortly after he returned home he died of a sudden coronary infarct.

My father, who I loved but had never been allowed to fully understand, and who had hurt me deeply a couple of times, without intended malice I'm sure, was dead just as true communication began to seem possible. As usual this gave me leave to blame myself for the past and not putting into context his visit to his old school.

On my visiting some months before mother had asked whether I had noticed the leather strap on his wrist. I had noticed but not mentioned it knowing he would have shrugged the question off. She told me he'd hurt his wrist and forearm somehow and Reg next door had suggested the strap. I knew I should have questioned him anyway as it now seemed obvious that the left forearm pain had been due to angina and with an answer or two I might have been able to persuade him to consult a doctor. I'd never known him to involve a G.P. in his life and as the death was sudden an inquest was ordered, ischaemic heart disease being the verdict I then felt sure of the angina and cursed my reticence.

Al's heart condition had been deteriorating for some time and it took a sudden down turn on holiday at Eastbourne. His mother Phyllis joined him at the hospital and wrote to tell me the news and to say that I could get updates on his condition by phoning Jon his brother. I learned that there had been no change on a couple of calls but then that he was dead. I don't know how I responded to Jon 's sad news, but after hanging up I screamed and blasphemed challenging whatever cowardly 'brute and blaggard' if one had indeed made the world to face me, to let me have my say and then, if he chose to, strike me down. I left the phone box and wandered around the streets until calm, then went home to break the news to Estelle. Then two of us were distraught.

Two giant presences had gone from my life and the lives of others over the course of a few months and yes I felt for Al's family and friends also for Mum and those who loved my father but I freely admit I felt sorriest for myself. Could I have done more, should I have done more? Would Dad have listened had I made an effort to get him to a doctor? Should I have gone to Eastbourne, at least I would have been there when Al reached the end?

Later after Al's funeral Phyllis told me that Al had hallucinated horrible and frightening things before his death and had begged to have his bed pushed outside into the open air, a request denied. She further told me that even had he survived he would have been required to use a wheelchair and how much he would have hated it.

As Dad lay at the funeral parlour, me, my cousin Mark and brother Syd were asked if we wanted to see him, I said no, I preferred to remember him as anything but a pathetic attempt at a facsimile and we left. Later the other two told me I shouldn't have said no as they both wanted the opportunity. I suppose I should have felt a measure of contrition but instead I felt puzzled amusement, had I been the spokesman for the three? Surely the eldest, Syd, should have been that; as the question had been greeted with hesitation I answered for myself and they should have done the same. I said no thanks, they should have said yes please!

The first to have left our alliance of friends had been Tom S who was a cheerful but not particularly articulate member of the gang. In our discussions as a group his contributions were few and far between, he might interject that he didn't agree but when prompted to explain his position would only repeat he didn't agree. How and when he dropped out of my orbit is a mystery. He didn't share our interest in folk music and I assume we gradually went our separate ways. Steve H. bought a motorbike and the last time we all went off together on the Easter bank holiday to Malvern I'd asked him if he'd fallen off yet and he'd sneered at me. Just as we turned a sharp corner with Al and me in the Isetta and Dave behind he fell off in front of us, going very slowly so no damage to him or the bike but as he got up rubbing his thigh with his other hand he shook his fist at me. One week's holiday together later as part of the group and then he too slipped into the past.

Once I married and moved away John K also left my orbit although I bumped into him once or twice over the years when back in Coventry but problems within his own marriage had driven him to bitter denunciation of womankind and our lives and thinking had diverged too much to reconnect. And Phil M I last saw at Al's funeral. Memories of him are tinged with amusing incidents, such as how he invariably walked a few paces in front of us perhaps embarrassment urging him to keep his distance, and leading Al to mouth to me 'Philip's the pathfinder.' And when giving a party for his work colleagues refusing to invite us because he didn't want us spoiling things as these were nice people!

Al was presentable in any company whereas I, as Michael Atkins had once confirmed, was liable to Rabelaisian discourse once among friends and as capable of being anything other than 'nice' as the following reveals.

Someone gave my father what they described as geranium seeds, more precisely pelargonium when he described what he expected to grow. Sowed in an old clay pot of garden soil taken from the rockery and left outside to germinate I was confident that a lack of success was guaranteed but after a few weeks seedlings appeared and once a few days growth I could tell what they were and told him. He took a look and said I was wrong these were definitely geraniums. After a month the pot and rapidly growing young plants suddenly vanished. They had been as I'd told him weeds, namely docks. That leads me to confess a mean-hearted thing I did, one of those deeds that you wish you could undo.

Chapter 33

A couple of years later someone, probably the seed donator tried again making him a gift of a number of rooted pelargonium cuttings which he placed behind glass in the garage window and promptly went off on holiday with Mum. This was the first time they left me on my own at home and I was pleased to be trusted. He didn't ask me to look after the cuttings and consequently they died from lack of water, even as they died I knew I was at fault but left them just the same. For reasons that are obvious to anyone who has read this far I needed a measure of revenge and the temptation proved too strong.

When they returned I saw him glance at the garage window in passing but neither by gesture nor speech did he show his disappointment, but oh, the regret and guilt I felt.

My old mate Jim Cooper who, after school in Davos Switzerland to help his asthma had come back with an interest in mountaineering and first aid. He became a probation officer and took an interest in the problems of youngsters and probably also mine although we never discussed the issue. How much he understood of my physical problems I don't know, although this next episode gave me more than a clue. He had a land-rover and asked would I like to go with him and a group of young people up to Corley Rocks which we knew well from school. They were practicing abseiling and after I watched for a while Jim asked would I like to try.

The answer had to be no thank you. I had enough problems walking on the flat and I could tell from observation that the unaccustomed strain on elbows and knees would have caused a bleed and remember I had no easy access at that time to plasma let alone the not yet available clotting factor. On turning the opportunity down my emotions were very mixed, on the one hand I felt embarrassed to have to say no, appalled that someone I'd known so long, though perforce on and off, could even ask but at the same time elated that my problems were not so noticeable as to make me an obviously disabled person. Only later did I see that he was testing to see if it was a good idea to ask me to join the climbing expedition to Norway that he and the kids were training for.

Why he bothered with me I must put down to his memory of our long association from pre-school days. While I once sang with him at a Red Cross event and we met occasionally thereafter I never felt fully comfortable with him on his return from residential schools on the Isle of Wight and Davos. Analysing from where I am now I see that with my need for continuity I had felt deserted and, possibly, resentful. Unfair, he did what he was told and what was best for him, and any negativity I felt could only be selfish. He had also taken up parachute jumping, sky diving perhaps, and landed on a roof from which he fell to the ground breaking both ankles. I knew, but I never went to see him once although he was confined to the house for some time.

I had become gradually more tentative both with family and old friends, not wanting to impose on lives which I felt could well do without my input. Patronage and nagging could also be avoided by keeping a distance between.

Over a few recent years I tried to find him and renew our friendship by apologizing for my selfishness and neglect of what should have been an obligation. His parents were dead and the house sold. Not having made any effort for years I knew no one who could have helped and tried all the social media available to a PC user. I found someone who'd lived close by and who remembered the family but could give me no information. Then I found him, in the local newspaper in the deaths column.

I attended the funeral and learned that he had been ill for quite a while with a degenerative neurological problem and wouldn't have known me even if I'd managed to find him before the end. Salutary was the fact that his surviving siblings didn't remember me either, just what I deserved!

As to my closest family, some years previously Rosie had settled down and was, while not a paragon of virtue, more tractable and she and her boyfriend married and for a while lived quite close to our home until moving to a house off Clay Lane.

Here they acquired two dogs, Bilbo a Jack Russell and slightly later a cairn terrier, Wallace. These two were later joined by a stray bull mastiff that they kept and called Ben. So three dogs, and all three were lucky not to be named Barry as every other animal that entered the house found the name foisted on them. One I remember was a little owl. Matt worked at the Combe Abbey Bird Garden and brought the owl home with him for some reason, he also brought food for it as he'd been instructed, a frozen sheep's head. This, still frozen he placed in the cage with the puzzled bird. A while later it was remarked that the bird wasn't eating. The thing in his cage did not truly resemble a sheep's head but I'd said nothing, after all who knows what had been done before it was frozen and perhaps that's how they always looked. As the frost melted I realised the silly mistake, the head was inside a plastic bag. How this blunder was rectified I don't know as we took the option to make an excuse and leave.

Perhaps calling a frozen sheep's head debacle culinary by inference is talking things too far but the next culinary disaster fell on Matt. We arrived just in time to disturb the evening meal, smoked haddock; undeterred by the dogs and our gaze he carried on eating or attempting to eat. Valiantly tackling the fish, knife and fork strained to breaking and tried to chew what looked like a rubber spoof. When asked the puzzled question 'How did you cook that, Rosie? Equally puzzled she replied 'What do you mean it doesn't have to be cooked, it's smoked.' We laughed and gave her the truth, thankfully the couple laughed too.

Matt and I shared an interest in wildlife and took a couple of trips together, one a long walk and the other a journey to Shropshire for a couple of days camping and nature watching. We set up camp in a field at Ratlinghope, pronounced ratchup, for which we paid a small fee, and had the whole field to ourselves. Immediately we glimpsed a honey buzzard and couldn't believe our luck a lack of belief confirmed as our sceptical eyes saw the same bird emerge from behind a hill full of trees and soar above us, a common buzzard. After this we laughingly claimed all buzzards to be little honeys. We did see a number of black tailed godwit land in a marshy field and up on the Mynd a raven or two, red grouse and curlew and heard them over and over, quite a noisy environment for a place where we saw no other person.

Later we visited the Stiperstones, Matt walking and me struggling to get as near to making a climb as possible; quite soon I was forced to admit I'd reached my limit, always remembering I had to walk down again and Matt refused to carry on to the top without me. He needn't have worried I anticipated disappointment in such situations, my goal being to achieve all that was possible not the impossible. Oh, how I dislike that song; any fool can dream the impossible dream, real wisdom and courage are needed to discern and attempt the possible dream.

Walking down, when I could walk, gave me more of a problem than walking up. Unless the muscles gave out I could carry on for a worthwhile time especially with a target in view, be it a boulder, isolated shrub or the top of the hill. Coming down put strain on other muscles and the knee joints and could be perilous as the difficulty of holding back threatened to force me into a headlong run. If I'd allowed the situation to deteriorate to that extent the only recourse would have been to collapse down. If I could make it to the target boulder of the assent then I could perch for a few minutes, this, a tussock or any other irregularity noted on the way up would become a staging post on the way down. The physical and mental strain cannot be over emphasised but the reward of achievement driven only by the self and the opportunity for contemplation of the wider view and the close scrutiny of flora and fauna missed when striding past was immense.

We drove all over that part of Shropshire bounded by Ludlow in the South and Shrewsbury to the North, mostly taking B-roads and lanes with Matt reading the Ordinance Survey maps. After a walk along part of Offa's dike we crossed into Wales and in Montgomery bought the most disgusting fish and chips I've ever tried to swallow. So powerfully bad were these that the memory is all I have of Montgomery. Some years later, talking with Emma she mentioned that on a walking holiday with her ex-husband they had experienced the vilest apology for fish and chips and yes, we had in common that these had been bought in Montgomery!

Our most dangerous moment came when we took the steep descent off the Mynd where somewhere between Cross Dike and Devil's Mouth with a sheer drop on the left and a rock face on the right the thought of meeting something large coming the other way suddenly occurred to me and sure enough round the corner came a removal van.

33

This was certainly large and there was no chance of either vehicle turning back, well in retrospect perhaps with a bit of careful manoeuvring I could have got the mini turned but it looked to me that there was enough, just enough, room for both vehicles to pass. Matt wound down the window and stuck out his head while I concentrated on not scraping the van and we inched past with Matt telling me OK, there's still room. Once past he told me that at one point only six inches separated us from a rendezvous with the rocky terrain a hundred feet below. Thankfully we made it without startling the few sheep precariously grazing; the poor things had problematic lives to contend with as it was, our screams and the crash bang wallop could have sent them into a panic.

Our next and final trip took place around Henley in Arden. Looking back from where my mobility is now I can hardly credit the fact but tracing the route on the map it looks as though we covered roughly six miles give or take as I can pinpoint where various incidents took place even after twenty -five years or so.

We parked in Henley close to Beaudesert and started the walk by taking a look at the motte and bailey site then taking the right of way across fields and lanes to Preston Bagot, a short walk along the road then we crossed the A4189 and down to the towpath of the Stratford canal then up onto a lane just before a bridge over the watercourse that joined the river Alne shortly thereafter. Standing on the bridge we looked down and were rewarded by the sight of a water vole swimming across and the sudden brilliant flash of a kingfisher.

Back on the footpath we crossed a field to follow the course of the Alne through more fields and stopped to rest on a stile between two. A well tamed hawthorn hedge ran both sides of the style and something was approaching from the left along the hedge bottom. Suddenly out popped a stoat, chattering and snarling, made a semi circle round us, right out in the open, offended at our temerity in blocking the accustomed progress of a wild beast, then back into the hedge to continue his journey. We too continued ours, across more fields to Blackford Mill farm and then back into Henley. The walk along the main street was torture for me.

I had reached the end of my endurance although I had followed my practice of sitting for a couple of minutes on any convenient perch or improvised seat but along that road there wasn't even one object my innovative mind could discern. The muscles in no time were trembling and I was in danger of not being able to lock out the knees, the only welcome but unsatisfactory respite was gained by leaning back against the wall and standing on one leg then the other which allowed me to walk on a little further before having to repeat and repeat until we reached the car where I collapsed into the seat.

I had only been able to walk as far as we did on that day as I'd gone some time without a knee bleed which always took it out of the muscles as I needed to take it easy for a while and the muscle mass was hard but smaller than it should have been because of all the serious knee bleeds in the past. If I'd avoided knee bleeds for some time then I could walk fairly well and if chance provided me with a log, style, bench or whatever for frequent rest quite a distance could be covered.

The couple eventually split up and though I visited Matt and his new girlfriend after he moved to Birmingham the relationship dwindled to nothing.

Rosie found herself a new boyfriend, Steve, and they produced a daughter Eva. I got on well with Steve but their relationship broke down not long after Estelle left for pastures new, and Rosie found yet another male friend. I was not certain of Luke from the beginning; Steve was unpretentious with no claim to superior intelligence. Not so Luke. He talked as though he knew what was what but really didn't but then I had no reason to be irritated I just was.

Suddenly they appeared to have decided on no further contact, which surprised me as Rosie had once sent me a card telling me I was a great man. I can only assume that the dislike I felt for Luke was reciprocated.

Other friendships and associations came out of the involvement with writer's groups some fairly short lived and others more enduring, also a few poems that I recall out of a great number produced, I no longer have copies of any of these and never learned them by heart, only to be expected I never learned any of my stuff by heart but here are the titles less the authors and in no particular order. Across the Barrier, The Gift, Coffee, Baudelaire and Sunday Fathers, I'm not saying these were the best just the ones that gave me enough pleasure at the time to be remembered with gratitude.

Mal of Southfield Writers was ever cheerful and knew his limitations, I think he was dyslexic, the word was never mentioned but it was obvious from the sometimes hilarious mistakes he made. Lower case n and u were often confused as inverted they look identical and at other times phrases but never, thankfully, whole sentences would be unreadable.' Limped wothers' had me stumped until the context revealed the clichéd meaning limpid waters and as to the membership list he produced for CWA!

The remembrance of this list and the misunderstandings generated provides amusement to this day. We had been sending material to a Mrs Middage for about a year before a non-member who knew the lady informed us that her name was Mary Dadge and another poor man had been receiving his addressed to Manrice Rathgun who I assumed hailed from the Caribbean but who was of Irish origin in fact, Maurice Rattigan. Most of the other dyslexiconisms were obvious and corrected, people resurrected to groves who had been placed in graves for instance but my own blunder consisted of an apology I sent to Ted Womble for making such a mockery of his name only to have him reply that he was in fact Ted Womble!

Always willing, if not always competent never upset by disapprobation Mal was a pleasant man, although I was once asked why do you bother with these people? The answer was that he was indeed pleasant, interestingly eccentric and friendly. His eccentricity was also evident in his appearance, balding head, and suit jacket lapels liberally sprinkled with badges and very close fitting drain-pipe trousers. We lost touch once my involvement with the community writing scene came to an end.

Claire I have managed to keep in touch with and she visited me just a couple of years back and later sent me some of her poems. She was one of the founding members of Southfield Writers and demonstrated the good side of community writing and community arts in general. I numbered her among my friends where others were only acquaintances and I appreciated her ability to think for herself and not to be tied down by belief. I recall with nostalgic pleasure how we once went to the cinema and saw My Beautiful Launderette, also the times when I gave her a lift home and we would chat for a while sitting in the car before we went separate ways.

Married with children she had decided on changing her life by going outside the family. She had a lover as well who lived not far from my address and would often call in after leaving him and on her way home. We talked about so many things and although attracted to her I made sure I didn't interfere by trying a seduction however delicious a prospect, life was complicated enough for us both.

I did interfere in her love life but that was at her prompting when all three, Claire, me and her lover were at a party together. She would have liked to move in with the man but he had kept her hanging on for an unconscionable time, content with sex without commitment. In front of him she asked what I thought of his behaviour. I confess to have downed a little alcohol and my facetious, mischievous side was on display, in stiff formal tones I hit him with the archaic 'You Sir, are a cad.' no laughter was forthcoming and he looked thoughtful. Later I was astonished to hear him say he'd considered what I'd told him and he quite agreed and was determined to do the right thing. A silly joke had been taken seriously and I had failed to take seriously my friend's requested question. Did they get together; did the cad fulfil the obligation he'd accepted? He didn't and it looked like he never would. Then Claire asked me another question.

Having met someone else what did I think, would moving on and sharing a life with this man be for the best? I hesitated for a few seconds as possible ramifications jostled with what business was it of mine and then told her to go ahead if she thought it would lead to her greater happiness. She and her new man, likeable and lively, set up home together.

On one of her visits to my home she complained of a swollen calf muscle and I suggested she see her GP, she did and he said it was a bruise. Next time she called in the swelling was worse and there was pain but no tenderness, with reddening of the skin. I was uneasy and suggested another visit to her GP. Again she was told it was a bruise. Some time had gone by and being a haemophiliac I knew bruises and this wasn't one but, I believed, a more serious problem than mere surface bruising. With no history of trauma I made a guess which I kept to myself and asked her if there was another more up-to- date GP at the surgery and if so to see him. There was, she did, and the diagnosis was, as I suspected, DVT, deep vein thrombosis, treated she quickly recovered but left any longer, already it had taken too long to diagnose, it quite possibly may have led to death from pulmonary embolism.

Chapter 34

Congratulations to the doctor who had the sense and courage to challenge the misdiagnosis of senior colleagues, to hell with protocol, and congratulations to self for the practical use of arrogance and experience.

Carole I met through Malt Shovel Writers and liked her immediately finding her attractive in every way. Divorced with two daughters to care for she coped very well with her situation was politically aware and fully engaged with the world, at least as far as family commitments permitted. In my mind, I see her in front of me head thrown back with a chuckle, when other faces and forms are lost in the hazy past. I would have liked a closer relationship to develop between us but having lived through Rosie's rebellious teens and Demelza's shenanigans I had developed a deep wariness of female children, besides who knew what a disaster for all three, who seemed to be coping, the introduction of a haemophiliac topped up to the brim with a toxic mix of self-doubt and arrogance would produce. My various relationship breakdowns had left me with fear of further emotional pain but a greater than ever fear of becoming the vector of pain to others. Her friendship meant a lot to me before and after getting together with my son's mother but we gradually lost touch as both moved on from the community writing scene and my problems with the hip and then both knees leading to the subsequent loss of mobility and giving in to wheelchair use, something tantamount to defeat, I became heavily involved with disability oriented groups and individuals.

Coventry Council of Disabled People, Outsiders and of course Lesley, who once accompanied me to a party at Carole's where I met up again with Claire and in conversation we were able to catch up on the progress of our lives. I didn't really get to talk to Carole and was aware that Lesley didn't feel particularly comfortable, in retrospect my fault as I should have realised that although I knew her as very outgoing, confident and happier than I in a crowd and expected her to be her usual self, she was now outside her comfort zone with people she didn't know.

For those born with, or the potential to develop, a chronic illness bravery helps though not as much as the sillier Ablebods suppose 'how brave' they coo as someone applies themselves to getting the most out of their day but what's the alternative, give up?

Endurance and determination to make the best of yourself, not as you might have been if your genes had been kinder, but as you are; acknowledging your limitations while making sure you overcome them count for more than bravery. In the words of the song "It's not just what you're born with but what you choose to bear'. Lesley chose to bear her physical problems, enduring the downturns in her condition determined to live the life she had made for herself with, yes, bravery, humour and care for others.

Unfortunately a totally unconscious prejudice lurks under the surface, a wheelchair user tends to be recognised on those terms first, the need to categorise newcomers is an unfair tendency of us all, to a greater or lesser extent, and disabled people have to work harder to be accepted as worthwhile members of the crew. Wheelchair users are thus unintentionally disadvantaged, often referred to as wheelchair bound; as a wheelchair bounder (and cad) myself, being bound to the thing is not something I've experienced or would want to......then again, in certain circumstances, I'll try anything three times.

I met up with Carole on a couple of occasions but our lives had diverged, Carole was involved with Greenpeace, busy with campaigning and had a horrible health issue of her own, inner ear disease, to deal with and somehow I let a real friend slip out of my life.

Adrian was a valued member of both writing groups and when he first joined Southfields and malt Shovel was the subject of much speculation among some other members. I felt that he took pains with his poetry, a salutary lesson to some of us, and was serious about improving his technique. I sensed a need for privacy or reticence about his past so never questioned him. One obvious indication of his wishing to keep his private life separate was his insistence on a pen name, Liam

Martin, chosen partly because of his interest in the poetry of Yeats I felt.

Much of the early speculation surrounding him was down to the fact that we had a number of gay writers and hangers-on gyrating around both groups and probing questions geared to the task of ascertaining sexual preferences were the norm, and of course some were just plain nosy for any detail. I had been subjected to a number of what my inquisitors believed to be subtle questions concerning my sexual orientation by one of the sillier types. It's my practice to wait until a person wishes to tell me anything, including relationship matters, rather than asking. I know this can lead to the conclusion that I don't care, but if that's how I come across, tell me that; it's the least a person can do for both of us.

Sexual matters have never been raised as a subject for discussion between Adrian and me in any sense, itself strange as sex has strutted the stage with me throughout the farce of my life often leaving me with only a supporting role! I do remember his relationship with one lovely lady back in the eighties but we never even spoke of her.....

Although he left the midlands moving to the south where he has conscientiously worked in social care, one of the most demanding jobs, for many years since the writers groups days we have kept in touch.

Viv Stafford continued to be what I chose to regard as a friend from Coventry Writers Association onwards although someone once told me that I didn't want to know what he said about me behind my back. This person was quite right I didn't want to know. I did know

Viv and that he talked behind my back was not unlikely as he talked derisively about so many. He could be both kind and generous and on our electric kettle breaking he bought us a new one and stood it peeping out of its box with eyes, a tear and downturned mouth drawn on stuck on labels and with the legend 'give us a home' written on the box, rang the doorbell and drove away. Inside the box were replacement labels to turn the downturned mouth into a smile!

Viv Stafford, tall and lean to skeletal later, sometimes bearded and or long-haired and with an enigmatic, forceful presence was what is often referred to as a one- off. He could be, yes, helpful and supportive bur cruelly sardonic and irritatingly persistent in his opinions with many imperatives on how the others in his life should live theirs. Perhaps our friendship, if that's what it was, endured its trials because we shared some of the same traits. He would bring me amusing tales of the perceived folly of others and occasionally bring such others to meet me.

One of these, a woman, he'd warned me was so strange as to be what he considered the victim of mental illness. She turned out to be mostly nervous and obviously neurotic, not as mad as he'd led me to believe but given to fanciful ideas and a habit of jumping up from her chair to wander round the lounge or look out the windows. They left and within an hour he phoned to ask me what I thought. I have no recollection of either the content of her fanciful ideas or of my reply to Viv, I would have been fairly guarded but I did agree that she appeared to be unstable. Where Viv and his relations with females were concerned I'd learned to take care.

Not in the least amusing but sad and doomed to failure was his attempt to encourage a young woman to get herself free of heroin addiction and the prostitution that financed it. Married to a husband also addicted and with a young son she was supporting all three. Viv showed all his usual persistence and a high level of genuine concern. He brought her to meet me and I found her intelligent, articulate, pretty and pleasant. I didn't enquire how they met or even speculate on how intimate their relationship but know he was trying to get her to leave her previous life taking her child with her and that she stayed at his flat for some time. Inevitably his plans came to nothing and we never talked of her again.

The red-rose pursuit of Wendy and a slightly later incident when he introduced me to someone at a party, then told me later he was dropping her as she hadn't the looks he desired in a woman both prompted my discretion when discussing with him his conquests real or potential. Early in our friendship he'd told me of the girlfriend who he loved and who had left him.

He claimed it was foolish of her because they could have had a good life together but she had blown it and lost him. I was amused and charmed by his unconscious arrogance. Overweening in his attitude to others, I felt he looked for confirmation of the correctness of his actions and attitudes from those around him never content to let people go their own way.

When I first met him he shared a house with Tony who appeared to have the allowed himself to fall into the role of dogsbody and was liable to be shouted for and directed by Viv to get this or find that. With Viv out of the room Tony told me not to be surprised if Viv dropped me and the rest of those involved in writing fairly soon. He'd shared accommodation with Viv quite a while and had seen bunches of friends come and go over the years, a new set arriving and being dropped regularly. This was interesting news, although open to interpretation; did Viv drop these friends or did they drop Viv? His overbearing persistence could be difficult to accept, as too, the need to discuss the obstinate failure displayed by one friend who rejected his superior wisdom. 'DH' says Viv 'we all know Tony's a Dill, but he said something interesting the other day.'

Chapter 35

What the reported something was I have forgotten revealing that my interest was in the relationship not the content of any laughable or relevant gem of conversation.

Not long after getting to know them both I arrived to be let in by Tony, Viv lying on his daybed, propped up enough to operate the keyboard on his chest, immediately took up his pet theme of the moment, trying to get me to buy a computer. He had some new gadget or other PC software to demonstrate as a persuasion and couldn't find it so yelled for Tony. 'Tony, what have you done with (whatever it was) you must have moved it?' Tony entered and denied moving it or even having touched it. 'I don't know where it is Viv; you should look after your things, shouldn't you?' I recall Tony's words, delivered in his northern accent with a slightly high pitched delivery, after many years, as they struck me as suggestive of kitchen sink wife or mother, I was addicted to television plays, and although I managed to conceal my delight I was in fact delighted.

Despite Tony's prediction, although many of the friends and acquaintances common to me and Viv dropped away our association continued, partly I suspect because he got his way over the PC when he supplied me first with an old one of his own and then one he'd put together himself. Equally important was his failure to get me to come off the Motability scheme and buy a second hand car of my own. This he never let go of giving me the same arguments and attempts at persuasion for years, with me countering with my reasons to stick with Motability. He liked a challenge and perhaps he thought he could wear me down over time, occasionally I let him win but never on the second hand car question. An associated suggestion I rejected was the taking out of a loan with which to buy the car and go on holiday or whatever other use I chose. He made it plain that he could get me a loan, if I didn't mind lying to get it. I declined not because I was dead-set against fraud, as my belief is that the system we live in is fraudulent along with all governments and their agencies, my reluctance was threefold. It's too easy to get caught with all the unpleasant consequences; others who might not be competent at evading discovery and who could try to coerce me into who knows what would be involved; I wouldn't like to have to pay the money back, especially at interest, thus becoming a voluntary victim of usury. That Viv felt he could get me a loan was due to the fact that the house he owned was now mortgaged and he had got himself a further loan by claiming to be working when in fact he was not, officially that is. He had an alias under which he worked but eventually lost his home.

Forced by ineptitude to rent, he eventually moved into an upstairs housing association flat on one of the least desirable estates and his phone calls were now full of stories of nieghbours who failed to take his advice, growing tired of verbally resisting and not answering his knock on the door needing a physical barrier as deterrent. Viv's persistence was not easy to endure and complicated by the knowledge that he sincerely believed that if you did as he suggested your life would be considerably better.

He had a physical problem of his own that he exacerbated by smoking, and at least two phobias to complicate his life. He'd an upper body stiffness that I'd noted from the start but not commented on; this got steadily worse over the course of the time I knew him until he revealed that he suffered with ankylosing spondiylitis (AS) a type of arthritis that in Viv's case affected his spine leading to less movement in his rib cage on breathing and the increased possibility of lung problems. Stopping smoking would have been self-protective but there was no chance of that happening. The first of his two phobias didn't help with his physical condition, medication phobia. At one point in our association he could only allow one commercial over-the-counter analgesic for the back pain and toothache plus a topical gel. He would have medication prescribed but his compliance was always problematic. One drug he avoided altogether was alcohol and yet nicotine was fine.

His teeth were a big problem as a visit to the dentist was out of the question as this would have been extremely likely to have led to medication

Viv's other phobia was debilitating and dependent on the weather. Fog was his big fear and he would phone me to ask what the visibility was like where I lived, although perhaps it was just to talk. His fear was quite specific; what was lurking in the fog, and was it approaching under its cover, he would be awake all night looking out of the curtains to see if it had cleared. His only relief was counter-intuitive; he would drive for miles in the fog, or drink coffee in a motorway services café. He had fixed points in the city scape which on misty days he could check and if he could still discern them then it was mist not fog. I don't know if he sought help, or if help was offered but I suspect not.

Viv's medical condition continued to deteriorate until he reached the stage of not being able to manage as just moving around his flat became very difficult. He had never thought of his increasing general tiredness, pain and weak condition as a disability but now struggled for money too as he could no longer keep his 'unofficial' job going. I persuaded him to apply for DLA as he became increasingly disabled. He applied for and got it only to complain that he was 'Now disabled, because of you!' To which I responded by pointing out to him that his financial difficulties had been alleviated and wasn't that a good thing. He sighed and agreed but his GP who had been involved had set social services on him. The flat and Viv had fallen into squalor by this time and he was moved temporarily to some kind of sheltered accommodation while he and the flat were cleaned up, he disliked the rules there and was glad to get back to the flat. Mobility was an increasing problem and when Lesley died I gave him one of her electric wheelchairs to use, someone else donated an electric scooter and all seemed well, but his situation deteriorated again and he moved into sheltered accommodation, a small ground floor flat. Pleased for him I hoped he'd now be able to sort his life into something resembling order. I was wrong.

I gave him a few weeks to settle in and get to know his new neighbours before a visit but before the buffer time was up I had a phone call from the warden of the sheltered flats to say Mr Stafford had been taken into hospital as his physical and mental state had deteriorated since he'd moved in and she had found him lying on the floor; he hadn't been eating or drinking and had stayed in bed since moving in suffering with panic attacks. She gave me the hospital details, and informed me that a social worker was trying to arrange some help for him after he was discharged. Next day, with the help of Michael my PA I went to see him.

He looked more skeletal than ever and very pale, he'd phoned me with a list of things he needed and these were purchased and taken in. I didn't stay long, I'm not a very good hospital visitor, I always feel uncomfortable and ready to go immediately I arrive and struggle to remain, finding conversation awkward, I have never been entirely happy on the receiving end of hospital visits pleased to see my visitors but just as happy to see them leave, so why should the role reversal not be difficult too? Before leaving as requested I loaned him ten pounds.

He asked me to buy a microwave oven and fridge/freezer and have them delivered to his flat. I ordered the microwave before learning that deliveries could not be taken in and that the housing association weren't prepared to accept him back as a tenant as sheltered accommodation wasn't appropriate and he really should be in a nursing home. The panic attacks had centred on getting out of bed Viv told me, every time he tried to get up he panicked, the fear being that he would fall which when in desperation he finally forced himself into, happened.

My immediate problem was the microwave, already on its way, I diverted it to a friend who needed a new one as my gift, the search for a very specific fridge/freezer I put on hold and other requests, I-pad, a big pair of earphones and a dongle he changed to a wireless keyboard, USB hub, a shoulder bag, nail clippers, bath robe or large bath towel, half a dozen more bags of sweets, a large bottle of Coca-Cola and a further loan of fifty pounds. Could I also go to his flat and bring his computer to him?

Once he had his PC he would reimburse me! Was I wrong to be sceptical about that, where was the money to come from? He'd told me he was' broke'. I was persuaded by another that with computer and sweets he would be within his comfort level and not concentrating on getting back out as soon as possible. In any case I wasn't sure that he would be allowed to have it with him.

I decided on a strategy to put to Viv on my next visit; when he came out of hospital I'd give him a day using extra hours for Michael when we would do whatever it took to help him settle into a sensible routine, and that I, or rather we, would visit once a week both while he remained in hospital and when back in his flat.

Before I could go to see him and discuss my plan someone from the ward phoned to say that he was dead.

Chapter 36

Not terminally unwell apparently, he had suddenly and quite unexpectedly died at one o'clock that afternoon. A curious incident that morning has the appearance of a signing off from Viv.

Late morning a heron landed in the garden and having a vague memory that such events had predictive power I went online and read that this happenstance presaged a death. I make no claims for the coincidence, but merely report what actually happened, leaving speculation or refutation up to others.

So ended the at times fraught association between me and Viv Stafford an eccentric with whom I shared laughter and mutual support. Most of his advice I ignored as it came as an imperative but his words on the people around us not having the courage to have children of their own when they reportedly criticised my parenting skills and the later reassurance when I told him I hesitated to challenge those convinced of the correctness of their faith were well taken. He reminded my arrogant side that no true believer was going to be swayed or pushed to doubt by anything I could possibly say.

Despite risking accusations of morbidity and gloominess I must point out how close to me the grim reaper has cut his swathe.

As one piles up the years it's a given that the stars that shone in the firmament of family and friends should dim and extinguish but from my childhood I've been aware. My own demise predicted, friends and fellow patients as well as a grandparent out in the' cold, cold ground', all noted and accepted. Over the years five, possibly six friends and acquaintances have taken their own lives, no blame attached to me though naturally I wonder could I have done more to help. Apart from the natural 'wastage' of old age.

Friends who suffered from chronic illnesses died too young and my loved partner too, on Christmas day 2014. When we moved into this bungalow in October 2014 Lesley and I had great plans for the place and a cat, Che, who caused laughter every day, now both are gone.

I'd be distraught if I thought his life with us had been anything other than happy, and I wish I'd known what had stressed him into losing his fur when the RSPCA first had him, if I'd known then I would have made sure I was not in danger of allowing the same conditions to occur. A visit to the vet as he was vomiting regularly meant daily tablets. At first we'd conceal the tablet in a piece of cheese moulded round it but this only worked a few times and then he would separate it and spit the tablet out. From then on it became more of a trial for us all. I knew the technique, how to open a cat's mouth with one hand and pop the medication in with the other but he soon came to resent it and we had to resort to wrapping him up in a towel like a mummy just to get to his mouth.

After some weeks of this he had made no improvement and with the vomiting getting worse the vet advised an exploratory operation although sure it was cancer and if nothing could be done the kindest thing would be to increase the anaesthetic and end his life. The temptation was to keep trying but if left any longer he would most likely have choked to death as it was becoming more and more difficult for him to swallow. Reluctantly I agreed.

The evening before his last trip to the vet he sat next to my wheelchair, purring, content not to come up to take his preferred position on my arms and shoulder.

I asked if I could be with him as he was prepared and given a tranquilliser but they said there was not enough room to accommodate the wheelchair. He trusted me completely, didn't trust the vet or nurse and I could have reassured him by my presence. It was not to be and if anything needed to show me that fully trusting another was a mistake that was it. I let him down.

The vet had told me it might not come to losing him but when she told me there was nothing to be done and I replied I thought that would be the case; she snapped at me that she'd told me it would happen. I didn't bother to argue that she had said it might.

He had loved playing in the garden when I took a long thin bamboo cane and rustled foliage or best of all a plastic shopping bag which he would pounce on thrusting his paws inside then run excitedly around the garden. His other vigorous activity involved running up a huge redwood tree the soft bark facilitating, to turn around and run back down leaping the last four feet then continue the run up the garden through the gate to come to a halt by the front gate.

Flora would often try to entertain him but I'm afraid he found her much too slow a companion, having to stop to allow her to catch up, then with a brief lick or two at his shoulder stroll off. As flora and I became ever closer she too proved an amusing companion.

Hilariously grabbing onto the closest veranda supports with one leg cocked in the classic pose adopted by cartoon character women confronted by a mouse, crying 'Whatever is it.' as the net I used to catch and release trapped butterflies fell from where it stood and whacked her on the backside. 'I thought it was Che.' she said though why he would do that she couldn't say. We both laughed and still do whenever recalling it, particularly the stereotypical reaction. Flora is the most easily startled person I've ever known, all sudden noises or motions liable to make her jump. A balloon bursting is sure to animate her and once at a football match where many balloons were released and stamped on, the veritable volley had her jumping around like a marionette manipulated by a demented puppeteer.

Her capacity for adding to the confusion of an already confused world is a byword at least as far as the two of us. It's easier for a passenger to get out of the car and fill the petrol tank than me and consequently when out together it's her job. For some reason on taking the ignition key, which doubled for the key to the lockable fuel cap, she misunderstood what I'd given her and sadly told me 'Sorry, you've given me the door opener'. I panicked temporarily thinking what have I done with the key and what have I given her, looking on the floor and in the ignition before I realised her blunder. Another amusing happening remembered with mirth.

These are a small sample of the comedy moments, she has even flinched on my arm being raised, if anyone saw they'd think I terrorised her with my violence, and once absent-mindedly broke a crisp in half and offered me, after careful scrutiny the larger morsel, another stereotype, her Scots ancestry showing?

Prevented by circumstances I won't divulge from living together she visits and stays every weekend, perhaps a good thing as the extended novelty keeps us loving the experience.

My appreciation of wildlife, birds in particular and of cats make for a lively time when balancing these elements.

A close encounter involving cat and fledgling proved the difficulty. I was aware that a lone cock blackbird was attempting to rear one fledgling in and around the garden. I was out there with Che and suddenly could hear the note blackbirds use to tell the offspring to sit quietly so looked carefully around and was shocked to see the young bird perched low down on a shrub just a few inches away from the cat's nose. I picked the cat up before he noticed and then had to work my way up the garden in my manual wheelchair while holding onto

Che, then devise a method of getting him indoors and shut in. Wheeling up the ramp to the patio door still carrying him was impossible so I opened the door a little way and shot him through the gap underarm, managing to shut it behind him just before he turned back. The cat inside and me outside with the bird, I had a further dilemma how to gain access to my home without letting Che out again, to ponder the point I went back down the garden.

The poor little fledgeling was now sitting on the ground trying to induce an aquilegia to feed it. This will read less ludicrous when you understand that the aquilegia was a first year seedling of the variety Black Barlow with a ruff of dark petals and a 'beak' that stuck out the middle. This plant bobbed forward in the breeze and to the chick looked much like its parent's head and with every dip of the plant it opened its beak and was disappointed to find no sustenance forthcoming. I left it there hoping a meal and a provider would soon appear. Having thought through my own problem I wheeled round to the front door and before Che reacted let myself in.

Both birds moved into a neighbour's garden so I never knew the outcome. With Che gone I have been expecting another cat to turn up asking for succour as three times in the past but so far no one has.

I have nothing against dogs as such but my own way of living and being in contact with others is more akin to feline than canine, dogs are pack animals, never truly happy when alone cats offer companionship only when to their own benefit and are therefore easier for me to understand. Not that I'm completely catlike in interpersonal relationships but that I lack the gregarious nature and need for leadership necessary to the dog. Florence my daughter's animal was a lovely, gentle soul long gone and still remembered with love but the only dog for me was Rover. I must be a one dog man. I have written about him previously in my book What Are Yer? Bleeder! Therefore just the one anecdote will do.

Chapter 37

Before my childhood friend Jim went off to school on the Isle of Wight he gave me an incredibly bouncy ball made up of rubber bands cut from cycle inner tubes. Rover who would spend hours worrying a large stone over next door's lawn or ours was out there chasing one around, head down at his front paws and behind up in the air, our lawn being unkempt it was impossible to see the stone as he knocked it and nosed it over the lawn. He eventually left the garden in his jaunty high energy way and later when I set out in my high energy way for The Dump and Cornfield I was astonished to see hundreds of red rubber rings decorating the path, borders, and lawn. Yes folks he'd demolished the ball to something no bigger than a marble, I tried to reassemble it but had not the power in my fingers or the patience. Was I angry? No, saddened at losing what was a high bouncing ball, a present from a friend and annoyed that I'd left it lying about but didn't blame Rover.

There are many who have not received attention in this book, who perhaps should have been included, neighbours friends and companions and indeed other bleeders, cousins and aunts and uncles. To do justice to all would require another two books and a whole lot more research than has been involved in this volume. However, two more characters must be included, my part in their stories being a mix of good and bad.

Outsiders member Sarah lived in a care home a few miles away and I received a letter from her asking would I like to visit, as a Birmingham lunch host I was happy to and met her at the home meeting other residents, staff and a few of her old friends too.

She used an electric wheelchair and had once married and left residential care and on becoming pregnant her sisters insisted on an abortion threatening to disown her. What her husband thought she never revealed, the threats worked and she complied. On her husband's early death she was persuaded back into the care home, her trusted GP also resorting to the application of heavy pressure by telling her he would not be responsible for her safety if she refused. These details of her past she told me, I have no way to check the veracity.

When I first met her she had a number of outside interests as a member of PHAB and attended Hereward College a couple of times a week. At that time the home had a van, employed a driver and a diary was available with details of who was to go where. On administrative change all this went.

Early on in our friendship the driver brought her to my home where I made sure she understood that my interest in her was not romantic and on that basis I would be around as long as she needed me. I knew she wished to find a partner and that's why she had joined Outsiders. I visited her regularly and she came to the Birmingham lunches. My visits were strange as she seemed content just to have me there and could be taciturn at times so that I talked more with some of the other residents. Then she had the luck to win a substantial amount on the lottery, not a top prize but enough to buy her own accessible van and a bungalow to move into. I visited her in her new surroundings two or three times but she was as silent as ever and appeared trapped, her carers not prepared to drive her out in the van. My own health giving me problems I wrote to say perhaps she could visit me and phoned a couple of times with the machine taking the messages but the next I knew her death announcement appeared.

No one let me know and I didn't attend the funeral, she had not complained about the level of care she had received but I was angry and didn't expect to keep silent. She had wanted to attend Coventry's Enterprise Club for disabled people and I had, at her request, phoned them on her behalf when the carer on duty at the time told me that she was the only one among them that could drive and that she didn't know her way around Coventry and when I suggested a sat-nav she said no it would only be stolen. Sarah said nothing. On lifting the phone to make the call hoping that transport could be arranged I discovered phone calls that had never been accessed going back some time. Before she died I had a phone call from the woman who ran PHAB to annoyingly ask did I know Sarah was now living in her own bungalow she seemed stunned when I told her I'd visited three times. It may well be true that I could and should have done more but apathy had taken control and I would have been imposing my will and wishes or so I felt.

I felt I'd done as much as could be expected by anyone even me and that I'd tried to help. In the case of Estelle's father I know I failed.

Charlie was a locksmith and veteran socialist, a member of SWP when I first met him; he'd been a member of a couple of parties in the past and had grown up in London's docklands. His father knew Lansbury and the family had accommodated Jack London on his visiting the capital. He had lost two businesses due to wartime bombing and worked at the Savoy as their resident locksmith, commuting from New Addington, Surrey into his eighties. Knocked down by a taxi with force enough to drive his tobacco tin into his chest leaving a livid rectangular bruise he nonetheless insisted on getting up the next morning and going into work. His knowledge not only of his trade but the intricacies, betrayals and personalities of movers in the working class struggle for emancipation was second to none. He could be blunt to the point of rudeness as when he told me it was about time I made my mind up which party to join.

Eventually he ended his life in care on going blind and I did nothing. I should have read at least some interesting articles onto tape from my socialist daily paper for him but didn't, a shameful case of out of sight out of mind.

Not much to say in my defense, its true I'd lost to death the three longest lasting masculine influences in my life, Dad, Syd and Al and no male person has meant so much to me since except my son but this is no excuse.

I hope I'm not stand-offish or aloof in my contacts with men but betrayal isn't the only vector of 'Never glad, confident morning again.' I believe it is true that as we age it becomes more difficult to fully enter into new friendships and I for one value old associations more strongly as time passes and the potential for new connections to develop recedes with my hair! Oh the fun of past time spent with friends, the holidays stuffed full of opportunity, the world a big and juicy oyster presenting itself for consumption and the pull toward ecstasy exuding from the feminine.

The silly girl who offered me the opportunity to fondle her not inconsiderable breasts if I paid us both into the cinema, and the Weymouth week when Al found a girlfriend and the rest of us didn't, I still in the grip of 'An old fever.' pulled about by need and what I felt to be ethics, the rest seemingly carefree.

Al's girl was on holiday with her aunt and uncle and they were very pleasant to all of us making no objection to her accompanying us as we drove around Norfolk in Dave's very crowded Reliant van, the couple cuddled up together she enjoying the back and forth flow of amusing and occasionally informative chatter.

At night all four young men crammed into the tent we'd made our way back to in the cool of the late evening and talked of many things before sleep. Typically I recall only one conversation, or diatribe and that instigated by me. Start from self (where am I) in a tent, in a field, in Norfolk and so forth until the universe is reached, then is the universe also inside something else, if not why not? The speculation could have been endless, ever expanding in fact but sleep intervened. I was proud to note that my friends got it, were duly impressed and delighted by a process I'd been through many times. The holiday over, the aunt and uncle shook hands all round and invited us to call on them if ever we were in their area of London.

We reached home and the three of us, our parents still away, needed to decide what to do with the second week. To me it was obvious, hadn't they invited us to call on them any time? This was a time and we had that time to spare! The madness of the idea enthralled and Al already missing his girl no objections were received so London Ho!

To say that the aunt and uncle were astonished to see us must be a given but true to their colours after informing us that their niece lived across the Thames in Greenwich they made up a bed on the floor of their sitting room and we stayed the night. Next day they phoned Naomi's parents and warned them we were on the way.

Made welcome by the family we slept in the van in their garden, eating with them and seeing the sights with Naomi as our guide. She had an older sister who told me she was jealous as her parents she was certain wouldn't have let her be driven about in a van by three boys. Later while in the kitchen the fascinating creature lost a false eyelash which fell into a sandwich she was making and had taken a bite out of before I could reveal where the thing had gone, 'I thought it was a bit crunchy' she replied with a laugh. Later she remarked mounting the stairs as I made for the van to sleep the sleep of the unjust 'I thought you were following me up'.

Chapter 38

Needless to say but when did that ever stop me saying anything, I would have been delighted but this was Al's show and it would have been several steps too far and perhaps have provoked a fierce reaction from her father.

The son of the house, a boy of perhaps ten years who came and went seemingly at will brought a lobster from a local market where he liked to hang out and concealed it in our bedding, a trick we all found outlandish but typical of childish humour. Quite a few years later a young man with the same name living in the same area was convicted of murdering a gay man in the local park, I hoped it wasn't he but thought it might well be. Al and Naomi kept in touch for some time by letter but as these things will it came to nothing.

Other holidays followed with other incidents including the sad spectacle of one friend, torn between need and ideals as much as I, conflicted by Roman Catholic indoctrination into yearning for a sexual encounter but unable to take the opportunity when it arrived. We took him to the fairground where if a brief encounter was what the old hormones demanded then gratification would almost certainly be possible but agitated and obviously torn, red faced he informed us that the girls all were all sluts, made an excuse and left. Empathy was easily aroused though my guilt and anguish was self-generated and not such a great preventative anyway. A sweet hour in a tent with a comfortable and comely female the best of my memories, though the details are withheld, the regret due to the enforced briefness of our collusion has never soured the memory.

The family friends and other bleeders who made it to these pages could be called the unlucky ones; many others escaped being exposed here. To any who feel grateful to have been left out and others who feel chagrined, a shrug of the shoulders! Enough words having been foisted on the reader already, besides cacoethes scribendi may strike again at any time. I have scratched the surface, an effective pruritus treatment for one who has lived life as a near death experience, over the course of the three books of which the present volume is the third and revealed what evil lurks in my heart. All three books are of course subjective and others may disagree with my revealed motives and my speculation as to theirs, if so I hope they read my books and write their own perhaps counter view.

Mysteries remain despite ongoing research; what is the Irish connection in my mother's family; is the story concerning Jim Kettle and his First World War heroism true; in which establishment did my great-great-grandparents fill the office of schoolmaster and school mistress and why has it proved impossible (so far) to find Frederick's birth and marriage records?

And so I have reached the end of this book and the long term goal of producing a biographical trilogy which while not comprehensive has mentioned most of what I feel to have contributed to a life similar to other lives but with additional challenges. While not seeking to suggest that my life and the lives of those who shared aspects of it with me has been vitally important I feel the three books tell a story different and complimentary to the history usually commented on by historians of various disciplines, the antidote to 'Everyone was doing this, or thinking that'. Individuals have a largely individual history and views on the history developing around them. Among people there is *no* genuine standard or position, assuming consensus as truth demeans the personal apprehension of the history one hopes to illuminate. An homogenized history ignores diversity.

I regret the necessity of leaving out so many who deserved mention, another sixty-five thousand words would be needed to include all. Any of my friends, family, enemies or those I met who feel let down or upset write your own history or contact me, but be quick – who knows when Mr. Reaperman may pay his inevitable visit?